WHITE WOMEN GETTING REAL ABOUT RACE

# WHITE WOMEN GETTING REAL ABOUT RACE

## Their Stories About What They Learned Teaching in Diverse Classrooms

EDITED BY

*Judith M. James and Nancy Peterson*

Foreword by Julie Landsman

STERLING, VIRGINIA

COPYRIGHT © 2013 BY
STYLUS PUBLISHING, LLC.

Published by Stylus Publishing, LLC
22883 Quicksilver Drive
Sterling, Virginia 20166-2102

Library of Congress Cataloging-in-Publication Data
White women getting real about race : their stories about
what they learned teaching in diverse classrooms / edited by
Judith M. James and Nancy Peterson ; foreword by Julie
Landsman.
   p.   cm.
Includes bibliographical references and index.
ISBN 978-1-57922-457-8 (cloth : alk. paper)
ISBN 978-1-57922-458-5 (pbk. : alk. paper)
ISBN 978-1-57922-909-2 (library networkable e-edition)
ISBN 978-1-57922-910-8 (consumer e-edition)
1. Multicultural education—United States.   2. Teachers,
White—United States.   3. Women teachers—United
States.   I. James, Judith M., 1947– editor of
compilation.   II. Peterson, Nancy, 1947- editor of
compilation.   III. Christianson, Bridget. Human error.
LC1099.3.W525  2013
370.1170973—dc23                                    2012039410

13-digit ISBN: 978-1-57922-457-8 (cloth)
13-digit ISBN: 978-1-57922-458-5 (paper)
13-digit ISBN: 978-1-57922-909-2 (library networkable
e-edition)
13-digit ISBN: 978-1-57922-910-8 (consumer e-edition)

Printed in the United States of America

All first editions printed on acid free paper
that meets the American National Standards Institute
Z39-48 Standard.

Bulk Purchases

Quantity discounts are available for use in workshops
and for staff development.
Call 1-800-232-0223

First Edition, 2013

10  9  8  7  6  5  4  3  2  1

*In honor of*
*Mary McLeod Bethune*

# CONTENTS

# ACKNOWLEDGMENTS

We are incredibly thrilled to have the privilege of telling our stories and offering other women the same opportunity. However, it is not an exaggeration to say none of this would have been possible without our superhero editor, Susan Carter. Her ability to streamline a wordy educator's tendency to overstate is nothing short of miraculous. What was most impressive about her editing is she approached the text with the sensitivity of a reader who expected to be moved and transformed by what she read. Therefore she kept us from gushing about our "exceptionality" and brought us back to the very human place where story resides—in being honest, vulnerable, and humble. This book is a testament to her generosity and exceptional work.

We were also privileged to have an advisory board that steered us in the right direction when this project was heading south. Thanks to Rae Cornelius, Linda Crawford, Ian Leask, and David Grant for finding our heading when the wind blew us off course.

Endless thanks to John von Knorring, president of Stylus Publishing. We wrote to him with our proposal, assuming two no-name teachers would not get the attention of a prestigious publisher or a publishing house like Stylus. Not only did John himself read our proposal, but he e-mailed us back within a week and called the next week. This is a man who must work 90 hours a week and yet spends his valuable time seeking the voices that are not being published. Thank you, thank you, John, for believing in this project.

And who gets so lucky as to have Julie Landsman write their Foreword? Julie is above all the teacher we all wish to be; she is present and generous with her time, and never, never, does Julie act as if she has the inside track on truth. Julie, you rock.

We also want to thank Aldon Tibbs, the handsome young man who showed sincere interest in our project and made sure our coffee was waiting for us and our cups always full as we pondered and planned the development of this manuscript.

Big thanks to our communities of friends who gave us support and affirmation and told us we were just plain stars to be doing this project. To our Friends in our Quaker Meeting, who encourage each of us to find our own voice and to look for that of God in each person.

This book is meaningful because of the tireless, often unappreciated teachers who work 60-hour weeks, spend a small fortune on supplies, keep coming back each year knowing the work gets harder, and believe there is nothing more important than to educate a child. Thanks to the teachers who made us better teachers and were nice about it: Eudene Lupino, Tom Noud, Rae Cornelius, Beverly Bennett Roberts, Mario Lee, Lisa McLeod, Marylee Johnson, Shirley Olson, RoAnne Elliott, Linda Crawford, Sister Maria, and Paul Murphy, the staff at Minneapolis Public Schools ECSE program.

## Judith's Acknowledgments

I thank my friends: Valerie Heffron, Kathy Anlauf, John Pikala, Harold Stone, Richard Seel, Dan Klas, Osla Thomason, Tamra Sharp, Linda Harness, and my international daughters HaeWon, Cemre, Ava, Nhu, Aya, Ayako, and Galit.

And my family: Jill and Jeff, you make my life interesting; Larry, you pay for my cell phone; Jennifer, you are one of those first-grade-teacher heroes; and Gisele Chauvin, what would life be without you in it? And my Godson, Frederic Rahgoshay-Chauvin.

Nancy, thanks for your faith in our ability to complete this book.

Finally, I dedicate this book to Lucille Marie Mangler James, a woman of substance who gave me the courage to speak honestly about all things.

## Nancy's Acknowledgments

I want to express thanks to Judith James, coeditor, who had the vision and passion to keep us focused and persistent in this project.

To my husband, Chester McCoy, whose love and support is always there, and to my daughters, Meghan Aisha and Hannah Jamila, who really hope we can get on Oprah and are going to start a website for the book. To my best friend, Annette Smith, who believed in me.

To my granddaughter, Esperanza, with the hope that she may find the culture in her future schools to be open, supportive, and creative in facing the hard issues before our society.

# FOREWORD

We study abstractions in our college and graduate courses—generalizations or ideas often without the vibrancy of concrete detail. Some of these ideas are provocative and they get us thinking or asking probing questions. Some generalizations come out of research and provide interesting perspectives on the way our world functions. The best of the more academic books, articles, and essays catch us off guard, make us look at the world from a new angle. Yet none of them stay with us in quite the same way as a rich story of struggle or trauma, enlightenment or failure. Because, after all, it is the story, the individual and complex interaction between one human being and his or her environment, that is universally compelling.

Thus, in an odd way, the idiosyncratic depiction of the events of one life, that one life's foibles and triumphs, often prompts a kind of universal recognition. This recognition has to do with the idea that we are all so complex—in our past experiences, our family life, and our separate and undeniable traumas, as well as in our economic, racial, and cultural lives— that to make generalizations about us is absurd.

Thus, the book before you, *White Women Getting Real About Race,* with its separate stories brings us home to recognizing the astounding variety of perspectives and life experiences that this group, any group, has. White women writing the chapters of this volume are so different, one from the other, so intricate in their knowledge and understanding, and so open in describing their failures and mistakes, that they present us with a panoply of experiences. And from this panoply we take a selection of lessons learned. We extract from each chapter things we can take with us and incorporate into our lives and teaching. We also come away with a new respect for the diversity among us White women and thus with a deep recognition of the diversity among and within any single grouping of human beings.

From the early childhood teacher to the college professor, from the high school theater instructor to the middle school English teacher, we learn how honest White women take from their experiences in education lessons about race, privilege, and running a classroom. Although each story is different,

*xi*

there are startling similarities, often around the idea of ridding oneself of presumptions, of the importance of assuming nothing about a being before you in the classroom until you know him or her well. Each writer in this book also makes clear that doing this work, taking into account White privilege and accepting that it exists, involves admitting mistakes, encountering painful self-knowledge, and plunging ahead the next day into the whirlwind of racial messiness again and again. We gather, by the time we have finished reading these narratives, that the work on Whiteness is never done, that new revelations come every day, and that the trick is to be open to those revelations. The trick is to lose defensiveness, gain confidence, and be ready for the next event that teaches a new concept in the artful negotiating game of education.

There is a cumulative effect of reading these stories, just as there is in progressing through a good novel with engaging characters. By the end of the book the reader gains a new respect, not only for these open and honest White women who are not comfortable with their privilege and struggle to address it, but also for the art and difficulty that the job of teaching demands from those of us who choose the profession of educator. And it is just this combination of story and focus on teaching that makes this book so rich, and so full of important information.

It is the myriad of voices, the collection of varied backgrounds, and the remarkable experiences so different from each other that make this book a real testament to those who struggle to make changes in the lives of their students and even in the communities in which they live.

Each chapter has much to tell us. And put together, all the selections in this beautiful volume have much to say about hard work, openness, a willingness to address race and privilege, and the persistence to go back, again and again, to struggle with these questions. One of the most admirable qualities I have found among White teachers, and in this case White women teachers, is their refusal to give up or to become overly satisfied with themselves. This is a tribute to the artistry of the profession, the amalgam of individual and community connections within the classroom that make it such a rewarding and tough job.

Each of these women is a self-reflective person. Perhaps, more than anything else, the cumulative effect of being in the presence of such willing self-reflection, and the innovation that comes from it, is the most important lesson to be learned here. It is through such reflective work that change is made, that progress happens. These White women show us how it can be done.

Julie Landsman

# INTRODUCTION

*Judith M. James and Nancy Peterson*

One of the most powerful social and political catalysts of the past has been the speaking of women with other women, the telling of our secrets, the comparing of wounds and the sharing of words.

—Adrienne Rich

The heart of this book is stories. We set out to collect stories of White women's experience with race in K–12 schools. We wanted stories that resonate with other White women and are not stock stories of heroic feats where we reign victorious.

We wanted our stories to smell, bleed, sing, cry, and rejoice. We wanted our writers to be brave and to challenge the racial status quo of color blindness and empathetic distance. We wanted to collect stories that don't use abstract educational lingo to separate us from the emotional cost of dealing with racism, White privilege, and fear of being racist in our turbulent yet rewarding daily lives in urban schools.

Our stories are written by insiders who are committed to engaging emotion, ideas, wonderings, curiosity, vulnerability, and reflective self-disclosure to expose the workings of White privilege. In our proposal for fielding stories we asked writers to ask themselves, "Will my well-being and sense of self be at risk if I tell this story?"

With these emerging/transformative stories we hope to challenge the security of silence by White women in schools. This silence on race binds each new White woman to a widening conspiratorial circle that reinforces silence as a protection against having to reveal our uncomfortable stories. Using stories, ours or their own, we want our readers to imagine and create a host of other educational possibilities as we build inclusive schools.

Recognizing what's at stake, we wanted our writers to be real with themselves. I (Judith) recently met an African American man, Walter, 47, who had been in and out of 14 different treatment programs over the past 25 years for a cocaine addiction. I was gathering information about his major losses—the death of his mother, the end of a relationship, alienation from his daughter because of his addiction, losing his faith—for a support group. What became apparent in our interview was that he had incurred a subterranean loss in his schools that broke his will to learn. He was told he was stupid for most of his school-age life. Of course he wasn't told this by teachers; it was his buddies and friends who humiliated him with words. The schools simply amplified his humiliation with special education classes, never explaining why he could read words but not comprehend them, and the outreach of unprepared educators who believed they were "helping" him. He graduated from high school and immediately began to fill his brokenness with cocaine.

Our stories are not told to overshadow the Walters or the Lucys (see chapter 2) of the world but to remind us why we must risk being vulnerable about our own ignorance. The women in this book understand the harm ignorance does and they signed on to be exposed. They were not only willing to be truthful in remembering their encounters with people of color but also recognize that the rewards of privilege allow us to keep our stories hidden, and to remain anonymous as we gain from that privilege.

The women in this book reveal their stories in hopes that telling them will help others to feel less alone, and then have the courage to begin a dialogue with staff and administrators to create a feeling of solidarity around race concerns rather than be solitary in intercultural conversation. It is not uncommon for teachers to experience the diversity training currently offered in schools as inadequate for addressing the reality of the urban classroom. Some feel caught with no support. The culture in schools maintains a hidden assumption that, once you shut the classroom door, you are expected to handle anything that comes up in that room.

Brenda, a special education teacher, suggested to the school administrator that teachers form small support groups to look at the dynamics between White staff and children of color. When this suggestion was brought to a staff meeting, it was presented as "voluntary support groups," with no mention of race. Unfortunately, Brenda felt too afraid to correct the administrator about the intent of the small groups. Brenda felt that, if in these groups teachers were to regularly discuss the impact of race on their teaching, such conversations would become routine and unconsciously integrated into the school culture. Instead, too often, teachers and teachers in training experience a diversity curriculum that is inadequate in addressing the reality of the urban classroom and rarely get support to figure out something more adequate.

It is not surprising teachers make cultural mistakes. We call these "excellent mistakes" because they have the potential to fuel honest dialogue and authentic exchanges if teachers can feel safe revealing them. Can we trust each other enough to open the classroom door and share our mistakes, offering each other support and real-world diversity training based on our own teaching experiences?

Many teachers we approached for stories expressed a desire to write their own story but were too busy running the marathon of daily teaching. Our hope is that those teachers and others will find a story here that resonates with them. We have included a chapter of exercises to use in small groups, staff development training, or alone at home for those White women teachers wanting to flourish in their classroom.

## Journaling

I write entirely to find out what I'm thinking, what I'm looking at, what I see and what it means. What I want and what I fear.

—Joan Didion

The writing process provides space, concentration, and introspection, in which the waiting mind may respond to the asking mind and carry our thoughts further than we could achieve in conversation alone.

—Christina Baldwin, *One to One*

The women in this collection of narratives have been able to explore their experiences to reach new levels of understanding through writing—one way to say difficult things aloud.

We recommend that you "flow write" in a journal after reading each chapter to capture your reactions—emotional, visceral, and/or intellectual. It is easy to "be in our heads" and to ignore our hearts, but it is very important to acknowledge the disturbances we feel and be grounded in our own experiences in order to make change. You will be surprised by what you find out about yourself.

Flow writing (also called free writing) is when you put your inner critic on a shelf, keep your pen moving, and write continuously for at least 10 minutes. But remember that the writing you do in this way, being honest with yourself, is very personal and can remain private if you wish. Say it first to yourself and then, if you are willing to take the risk, to others.

One way to see what you connect with, or what speaks to you, is to underline words that stand out for you as you read each narrative, then write from these. After you finish reading each chapter, flow write your own response to it. Then consider and respond to the Journal Questions at the end of the chapter.

*Bridget Christianson in 2009 when teaching
4th grade at Metro Charter Academy in Romulus*

# I

# HUMAN ERROR

*Bridget Christianson*

The chief cause of human error is to be found in
prejudices picked up in childhood.
    —René Descartes, *Discourse on Method*

## Growing Up White

I grew up in a predominantly White, middle-class neighborhood in suburban Detroit, where my dad was a factory worker. At his company picnics I remember watching him talking and interacting with his coworkers, many of whom were African American men. What I found fascinating is how he interacted with the guys he worked with—using the slang words and interrupted sentences, a strutlike walk, and a surly voice and manner. It was quite comical to me and unlike how he acted at home.

I was never of the opinion that my family was biased toward people of color because of my father's interactions with people different from us. Although my parents only entertained people like themselves, they never overtly referred to people who were different from our family in negative terms. My father enjoyed his coworkers; it was apparent in how he spoke about them. If I assigned any stereotypic traits to people of color it was because of how uneducated my father made his coworkers appear when he spoke to them using broken sentences and slang.

Besides that of my father's coworkers, the only African American behavior I readily observed was when watching TV. As a child, I remember watching *The Cosby Show* and *Family Matters* in the late 1980s and 1990s. But when I try to remember what influences those TV shows may have had on my life, I can't think of any. I didn't really see a difference between those families and my own. However, I do remember developing a strong distaste for the music I would hear African Americans play or listen to. It was just too loud and hard for me to understand.

If you were to look at any of my K–12 yearbooks, you would see a handful of students of color: African American, Arab, and a smattering of biracial students. But because there were so few, the idea of socializing with these students never entered my mind. I was with my White friends, and I never thought about whomever the students of color were socializing with—I just knew I wasn't one of them.

Because high school often emulates an organized caste system, I was defined by my friends just like everyone else was defined by their friends. The popular White students—students who fit the norm for being attractive, athletic, and sexually appealing according to White sensibility—enjoyed prestige and privilege, regardless of whether or not they were the brightest or the most benevolent. And, like the students of color, White students who occupied a position of disregard because they didn't register on the "popular scale" also socialized only with each other. Although we were all friendly in the halls and in our classrooms, as in most essentially segregated White schools, the rules and norms were set by the White students.

Were we racist? I suppose we were, but mostly we were ignorant.

## Pursuing My Dream Job

Ever since I was a little girl, I dreamt of becoming a teacher. In my dream, I would be the "cool" teacher, the teacher who made school fun and interesting. Students would approach me and ask amazing questions, and I would give them the tasks and the tools to discover the answer for themselves. The little girls I taught would want to be me and the little boys would want to marry someone just like me. I would be their role model for what an adult should and can be. I would take time and make sure every student was listened to and cared about and would make sure to see and treat each student as an individual.

My role models for what I thought a good teacher should be were the teachers I had in elementary school. Some teachers I cared about were funny. Some were tough but caring. Then there were the teachers who were just plain amazing. Each and every teacher I admired gave me gifts of knowledge and values, valuable and important gifts not just for learning math, science, and English but for living my life.

I also gained insight from a few former teachers about the kind of teacher I didn't want to be—the lazy teachers that I didn't learn anything from, the teacher who showed a movie every day and then gave a short quiz on the movie even though it was a composition class, and the ones that lectured for the whole class time while bored students openly dozed at their desks. These were teachers who seemed to talk just to hear their own voices.

I decided I would be a teacher who had all the good qualities and none of the bad that I experienced growing up. Staying true to my dream, I received my teaching degree in 2002 and set out to apply theory to practice, vowing to be the best teacher I could be.

## Coming Home to a New Reality

I was 21 when I started my first teaching job at Charter A, an elementary school with a diverse student population located near the same district where I grew up. I liked the area and the people who lived there, so there was a level of comfort in "returning home" to start my new career. In fact, I felt proud that I could come back to that district and have an effect on students' lives similar to the one my favorite teachers had on mine.

The first day of school was my birthday, and I loved the idea that my gift to myself was the beginning of a teaching career. "Happy birthday, Bridget! Your childhood dream of being a teacher is coming true." I was filled with excitement and enthusiasm about finally getting started. I felt inspired, was thrilled to be teaching, and expected it to be an amazing job that I would be amazing at, even though I knew it would be hard.

Little did I know how hard!

I knew I wanted the kids to learn from me, and I knew I had goals that I wanted them to meet. I brought with me high expectations for my class: to be well behaved, organized, orderly, and engaged. Unfortunately, I had *no* clue how to teach them to be that way. Perhaps the most disappointing realization that day was that, although I had expected my students to like me, I quickly found out that was not the case.

My birthday gift to myself wasn't that exceptional anymore. My brief time of euphoria was just that: brief. Then reality set in and I realized I would be at work all day and into the evening. The school expected that I would set up my classroom, make a year's worth of lesson plans, create materials for those lesson plans, and then figure out how to assess student learning.

The naïveté of my expectations was confirmed even further with the realization that the school administrators would give me little support or information that would assist me in those tasks. I was in complete shock when I exited the school on that first day.

It appears I came to work prepared to live the dream but unprepared for the reality. As a young girl dreaming of being a teacher, I never noticed how much work my elementary teachers took home during the week or over the weekend. I never realized how long they stayed after school getting ready for the next day's lessons. I never saw the time they put in.

Because I imagined teaching was like any job, except much more rewarding, I expected to go to work, teach the kids, do what the school wanted me to do, and then go home and enjoy my personal time—that I would live my life! That expectation ended before my first year even began.

I never imagined teaching would wring me out emotionally or constantly challenge me to find enough time for everything I had to do. My college courses and even student teaching did *not* prepare me for the enormous amount of time teaching took during both the school year and the summer.

## The Sixth Graders Take Control

To my dismay, fear was the driving force at Charter A. Other teachers said, "Unless they have the fear of God in them, they won't behave." They joked about corporal punishment. Occasionally, parents would come to school and take their child into the bathroom for a spanking. Some parents didn't even use that discretion and instead punished the student right in front of me and the class. Teachers, parents, and administrators repeatedly told me that the only discipline that worked was physical punishment.

The idea of striking a student was foreign to me, and I knew I would not use fear tactics or corporal punishment to get students to learn. I wanted the students to enjoy school.

Given that the school endorsed control and retribution, there were low expectations for performance. I expected each student to do their work and let the child and the parents know what major gaps the student had to work on. I spoke to one parent about his child's missing 76 assignments since the beginning of the first lesson, and the parent said, "Thanks for letting me know." The parent seemed hopeless and accepting of how poorly the child performed at school.

In an effort to gain an advantage over me, the children would often call me racist. When I tried to enforce any discipline the student would say, "You know, I can get you fired because you're racist."

There was no support from the principal or the parents when I attempted to enforce rules or curtail foolishness in the classroom. The climate of my classroom teetered on the brink of chaos because there were no consequences for bad behavior.

In one incident, an African American parent came into my classroom angry and upset. She stopped when she saw me and yelled, "My son said you had him stay in from recess for no good reason. He was the only one you kept inside, but he wasn't the only one misbehaving. So what's your side of the story?" The principal, who brought the parent to my classroom, stood there and said nothing, allowing the parent to yell.

With no inkling of support, I felt like I was living through the Inquisition, put on trial for trying to help her child. Perhaps it was my lack of experience, but I honestly couldn't understand why this parent would automatically take the word of her son over his teacher and not accept any rationale for why I did what I did. I could give her no response that she would accept as justification for my reprimanding her son.

I discovered that the parents also cared a lot about how other students in my class were punished; there was an assumption that their child was always given the greater punishment. At that time, I didn't know that equitable punishment is often a sensitive subject for African American parents. I just saw myself doing the right thing for each child, not trying to change the world.

Whenever I tried to explain what had occurred during and after an incident, the first thing a parent would say was, "What did the other boy do?" which was followed quickly by, "What punishment did the other boy receive?" What struck me as unfortunate is that the parent did not see a reason for his or her child to take responsibility for his or her own behavior. There was no accountability for the child's actions. The finger seemed always to be pointing outward at someone or something else. It was hard for me to see any part I might have played in the conflicts because I felt put on the defensive during every encounter.

## Working Within an Infrastructure of Nonsupport

The school was run by an ill-managed company, and any attempt to go through proper channels for assistance seemed futile. It was common practice at Charter A for parents to disrespect teachers, and teachers were cast as the villain or labeled as "mean." When a teacher filed a discipline report, the report sat on an administrative secretary's desk and then disappeared. Nothing ever happened with these reports; they seemed to evaporate as if they had been put into some hidden container filled with sulfuric acid. If I set up a parent meeting, parents wouldn't come and the administrative team accepted this behavior as normal. At the Knowledge Is Power Program (KIPP) charter schools, when parents and their children don't embrace the strict learning-only culture, they can be asked to leave. This is an option Charter A administrators never saw as viable.

Parents would endlessly argue with teachers about why an incident wasn't their child's fault. Comments made in justification of a child's behavior included, "My child has the right to hit someone if that person puts his hands on him," or "We will just go to a different school," or "It's not my son's fault if you can't control the classroom."

It was my impression that parents felt that if their child hit another student their child was utilizing a suitable strategy, and certainly an option that was acceptable in school. If any discipline was given for fighting, most parents ignored the significance of the suspension and allowed their child a vacation or shopping day. I never felt parents, the administration, or some of the teachers demonstrated an especially deep commitment to learning.

I admit making my share of mistakes. Interesting enough, even when I expected them to warrant disciplinary action, and they did, it never materialized. What the administrators cared most about was that I maintain order in my classroom. What I did or said to get that order didn't seem to matter.

I knew how wrong some of my behaviors were, but that didn't stop me. For example, one day I was teaching a compare-and-contrast story using a Venn diagram. To demonstrate, I used the names of my best friend, Jeanie, and myself, Bridget. When I put our names on the Venn diagram, one of my female students blurted out, "Jeanie, what kind of name is Jeanie?" Awestruck, I sharply turned toward her and said, "P'Sontia with a silent *P*, what kind of name is P'Sontia?"

The class chuckled, and even P'Sontia didn't seem all too upset by the comment, but I was disappointed in myself. I had embarrassed a student and felt awful about it. I felt like I had humiliated her in front of her peers using one of the most important tags for students: their name. That incident, above anything and everything else that would happen in my classroom, is what P'Sontia would remember from sixth grade—and from me.

Several times my ignorance—and that is what it was—shone through like a GloFish. One time in science class, we were studying static electricity. I was explaining the different charges between electrons and protons and how you could get shocked or your hair could stand on end because of it. Using balloons to demonstrate, I asked the students to vigorously rub the balloons on their shirts and then hold the balloons near their hair. Nothing happened. I didn't realize that it wouldn't work on their hair. So I did it to myself and the kids in class started laughing at me as my hair stood on end. Although I was embarrassed, the students did get a good laugh from seeing my funny hair.

Still, I struggled to achieve order in my classroom, and in January of my first year, my first principal (there were three in the course of my two years teaching there) told me I was "not mean enough" to continue teaching sixth grade and said I would be moved down to first grade. She said she would reinstate the previous year's sixth-grade teacher, who had five years of teaching experience at the school but no certification.

There was a teacher on my sixth-grade team who encouraged me to stay strong, saying "Don't let them make you step down." This teacher also had been reprimanded for the lack of discipline in her classroom, and when she needed support I befriended her through supportive interactions and curriculum.

Although I had found an encouraging ally, during my first year of teaching I was drained and in tears on a daily basis, with no fight left in me. Just getting through the year took every ounce of energy and courage in my reserve.

## A Better Plan for Year Two

Exhausted and discouraged after my first year of teaching, I agreed to teach first grade the next year. It struck me as absurd that it was a "demotion" to move me to first grade given the demands of new learners. If there were doubts about my teaching ability, why put me in a grade level that sets the tone for nascent learners?

Despite a rough first year and even through my worst teaching moments, I believed that truly effective teaching can overcome student indifference, parental disengagement, and poverty. But I needed to have some support. I was a first-year teacher, and I understood how naïve I was and that I was a novice educator, but there were no workshops, no evaluations, and no feedback or assessments of my teaching, for God's sake. The only advice I ever received was "get mean or get run over." For school leadership to just ignore the aggregate effect of student and parental attitudes on learning was reprehensible.

My frustration had escalated, but I would not let it consume me. I remained in teaching because I was hopeful that someday a leader would emerge and recognize the culture of the school and attempt to do something. I did not want to let go of my lifelong goal to be a teacher; I just wanted to be a teacher who felt good about what she was doing.

Over the summer, I took steps to better prepare myself for my second year. I reviewed my college textbooks and notes on classroom management and met with my advisors from college. I knew something had to change and thought maybe teachers who cared about me could help. My teacher friends, college professors, and family encouraged me to try new strategies and learn from my mistakes. They made me feel safe enough with my mistakes to talk about them and remember that making mistakes was all part of becoming a better teacher.

I talked to teachers from diverse schools who reiterated what I knew to be true: Treating every child as an individual and seeing the potential in him or her is more important than being focused on the ethnicity and race of a child. My teacher mentors suggested I not see learning and discipline as separate pathways in a class but that, through the establishment of standardized routine and well-organized learning exercises, I could integrate management and instruction.

My professors encouraged me to wrestle with the political and ethical issues present in the school and not give in to the status quo. I was encouraged to continue to reflect on my concerns about self-image, lack of resources, and procedures—not from the standpoint of a victim, as I had been doing, but from the position of a problem solver. For the first time since the end of the year, I started getting excited about how my classroom would be different in the fall.

## A New Beginning

My teaching and classroom management still left much to be desired during my second year, but with some strategies and a belief that I had a map for success, I did not experience the turmoil I had in my first year. I felt more in control and focused on what I could accomplish with the students instead of what I couldn't accomplish with them, their parents, and administration.

After I finished my second year at Charter A, I had an opportunity to teach at another charter school in the area with a similar demographic, Charter B. Joining Charter B was like moving to an oasis where everyone wants each child to succeed. The administrators, parents, and teachers set high expectations for every student and the children rose to meet those expectations.

In this new school, relationships are the key to success. It is the practice of teachers to work hard to build relationships with parents. The parents here don't feel negative about the teachers and would never think to humiliate a teacher. I have given out my cell number and let parents know I am available to support them and their children; it is more of a 24/7 job. We partner—parent and teacher—for the sake of the students.

In my classroom today, many of my White students befriend other Whites, and the Black students befriend Blacks, not unlike my own experience as a student. Beverly Daniel Tatum has written about this self-selection (or self-segregation) by students and about her belief that African American students are in the process of establishing and affirming their racial identity. As Dr. Tatum points out in her book *Why Are All the Black Kids Sitting Together in the Cafeteria?* students of color know they are "raced," but White students assume they have no race. It is my observation that most White students think nothing of "being with their own kind"; it does not appear to be a conscious decision for the White students. It's not that White students and students of color do not get along, but it is interesting to see who plays with whom during free time or recess and how social networks are set up.

I've grown as a teacher and I've also seen my interests grow, unmistakably influenced by my predominantly African American students. These ventures will seem insignificant to some, but for me they were steps into a land I had never traveled. Like basketball. I wasn't even interested in my own high school team; now I love basketball. I like certain musicians I would have never listened to, I can maneuver certain dance moves that would have been impossible in the past, and I am up on hip-hop and spoken word.

What has really been sweet for me is that students invite me to school dances, to their recitals, to travel with the city basketball team; they want me to watch them play football and baseball, cheer for them at competitions, and eat with them at the family barbecue. How different an experience it is to feel accepted enough that students share with me what they love.

I sit with students' family members at games and cheer on my students, who are very happy to see their teacher outside of school with their family. Families have begun to see me as someone who goes the extra step and who really cares about their child as a person. I have tried collard greens and sweet potato pie brought into school by students' families. I have even gone so far as to have my soft, fine strawberry hair braided corn-row style, just once. It was painful, but something I am glad to have done.

I realize that what happened to me over this time period is that I experienced ordinary living with a group of people I had never done anything ordinary with. I am reminded of something Kwame Anthony Appiah said in a recent interview on National Public Radio: "You have to come together in what I call—I use the metaphor of conversation. And the point about conversation is that it doesn't have a point" (Tippett, 2011).

The only reason I took risk of trying these new experiences is that I enjoyed the company of my students and their families. And, after seven years, I am still teaching in this school.

## Getting Real

Being real with the students brings me new life experiences. I am lucky.

Early on in my career, I was fearful of what I should do or how I should act, worried about being judged by parents and students. Now my fear has been circumvented by my desire to have conversations, new experiences, and create relationships.

I am more relaxed now as a teacher because of my experience and the changes I have endured: in grading, curriculum, how we score assessments, physical classroom location, administration, grade book, and more.

I know that I am not always going to be liked. I know that I may become "the meanest teacher ever," especially if I take recess away. But I also know that I am caring, understanding, and encouraging. My expectations are high, because I know my students can meet them. I know they can do it. I will help them, I will stand by them, and I will be their biggest advocate, because I am their teacher.

The teacher I always wanted to be now looks different from the one I had imagined, but I am that teacher. I truly do have my dream job and imagine myself doing the profound work of teaching for the rest of my life.

## Journal Questions

1. Bridget, like the women in many of these stories, wanted to be accepted and liked by the students. She found this kept her from setting limits and having firm and consistent discipline in the classroom. Journal about what needs arise in you when you are teaching.

2. Over time, Bridget shifted her orientation from victim to problem solver in her teaching. Journal, from your experience, what it is to play the victim.

## References

Tatum, B. D. (1999). *Why are all the black kids sitting together in the cafeteria? A psychologist explains the development of racial identity.* New York: Basic Books.

Tippett, K. (Host). (2011). Sidling up to difference [Radio broadcast episode; interview with K. Appiah]. In K. Tippett (Producer), *On Being.* St. Paul, MN: American Public Media.

# 2

# FOR THE LOVE
# OF CLOWNS

*Judith M. James*

"I knew I needed to journey deeper into my worldview to understand the picture of effective cross-cultural work—the hues, the form, the special qualities, the depth, and the smell of change—in order to elevate my work."

I knew, growing up in a military family, that worthwhile adults became someone's hero. In our family it made sense to give love instead of expecting to receive it, because our parents, particularly my mother, put their potentiality into their children, all under five years of age. My mother prepared Redbook meals, dressed us in freshly washed and ironed clothing, and educated us to be perfectly behaved children of God—all on my father's meager military salary. There wasn't the time, energy, or patience for emotional love. But to her friends my mother was a hero for accomplishing the difficult feat of presenting such a well-kempt family. Therefore, as a child, my image of love was to save people overwhelmed by their circumstances or living with great needs, and in return I would be their hero. As I grew older I was convinced by others wiser than me that wanting to save someone is paternalistic. But the childlike empathy for people hurting or in pain because they were unfairly judged or disadvantaged has been with me throughout my lifetime. My first recognition of this innocent empathy came on a road trip to my grandmother's house in fifth grade—four kids, a dog, and two parents, packed into our Pontiac Catalina.

## Discriminating Tastes—The Velvet Clown Painting

Like many children, I was drawn to black velvet paintings and the tactile pleasure of the fabric. My favorite was the image of the sad clown, who seemed scary to some children, but to me his distorted features were evidence of his vulnerability and a loveless life. Sold at roadsides and abandoned lots, velvet paintings seemed to pop up and appear around sharp corners on the highways across the Iowa landscape. Among the oversized velvet images of cowboys, Elvis Presley, and Native Americans, the clown stood out, sad and depressed. At the age of 11 I thought the melancholy, white-faced clown with the pear-shaped teardrops staining his cheeks desperately wanted me to care for him.

When I saw my first sad clown portraiture in a velveterian roadside gallery I pleaded with my mother to buy it. She laughed at me and said, emphatically, "No." Lucy was a woman with no patience for demanding children or behavior that went against the image of an ideal military family.

On a second trip to Sabula, the only island city in Iowa and my mother's birthplace, there he stood, my clown, propped up on the back of a pickup truck, proud and resilient. He reached out to me with those unforgettable black, pleading eyes calling for me to take him home. My noble prince, whom nobody loved, looked at me with those suffering eyes and mouthed, "Please rescue me, rescue me."

I begged my mother, "Please buy that clown for me? I will pay you back."

"You are not going to waste your money on that pathetic clown. We are not *the kind of people* who would buy our art in a dust bowl from roadside vendors, and our daughter isn't either."

My stomach wrenched. *What is wrong with her? Doesn't she see his pain? Doesn't she understand why I want him? He is an orphan.* I silently promised my troubled clown friend that I would be back with my babysitting money to rescue him.

At that moment I hated my mother for being so cruel and not understanding me. "This isn't the kind of people we are." I am one of those people, and I wanted that clown in my bedroom; I knew he needed me.

As I grew older in the middle-class suburb of Richfield, Minnesota, I grew into my mother's prejudices and learned who "those kinds of people" are, and how to avoid becoming one of them. I was in 10th grade by the time we took another road trip, and my childish belief about a certain velvet clown painting became a source of humiliation. As we passed the same highway stands I said with the overstated conviction of a recent convert, "Who are those ridiculous people with their shrine to velvet wall hangings here in Nowheresville? How sleazy—and look at that tacky-looking clown. Who would pay money for that vulgar clown?"

My sister snickered and then in a mocking voice said, "Oh that clown needs me, he wants me. Maybe he will be my lover." I shut her up by punching her in the arm.

Like my parents I wanted to project the image of someone who had *class,* and who wouldn't purchase her art at abandoned parking lots. I considered the "weirdoes" who were buying or selling velvet kitsch to be poor and unintelligent. Just as poverty and intelligence were forever linked together in the minds of my parents, I also unfortunately believed that being poor was being ignorant and that only ignorant people would hang velvet tapestries in their homes and call it art.

## Visualizing the Image to Be Put on the Velvet

I grew up in a developing suburb filled with German Lutherans who tended toward egalitarianism but shuddered at the thought of entitlement. Even though I knew my parents struggled financially to build a 2,000-square-foot split-level home, I, like they, felt we deserved it. My mother reminded us daily, "Your father and I have worked hard for everything we have, and believe me it wasn't easy. We never took a handout, never leeched off others; we made our own successes, and so will you."

Richfield High in the late '60s had cliques of jocks, nerds, druggies, and punks—in 1965 my preference went toward "Baldies," who wore dress shirts with a strip of fabric looped in the center of the back panel. The hip and those wanting to be hip proclaimed the Baldies as the ultimate in coolness. As cool as cool could be, we also knew the opposite of coolness was poverty. Students who hid their poverty in moderate dress and good grades were left alone, but we ridiculed poor students who "flaunted their poverty" by wearing "provocative" dresses from Woolworth or Naugahyde motorcycle jackets from Sears.

Even though I had abandoned the lonely clown from my childhood my feelings for those who were vulnerable, weird, or weak remained alive in me. I suspected if the popular students knew more about my family they would vanquish me to the painful unpopular club. This and my innocent empathy drew me to "those people" who were persecuted, and I defended them when opportunities arose. It was a character trait that mostly went unappreciated, but I didn't care because I understood the pain of poor children, including the Sharpe sisters.

The Sharpe girls were from "the other side" of Richfield, the east side. East-siders were the original Richfieldites; they came to Richfield because they couldn't afford a house in the cities. They wore clothes from Kresge's, and the girls teased their hair into a ball that sat muddled atop their head. The boys looked overtly sexual walking around with an imitation James Dean persona, in tight jeans and motorcycle jackets. I cared about the Sharpe girls, but they weren't all that enamored with me "getting into their business," and neither were my middle-class friends. When I defended the Sharpes my friends would say, "Why do you care who teases them? They're not your friends."

One day during the fall of my junior year I was taking a shortcut to class through the gymnasium and found four cheerleaders cornering the Sharpe sisters, pointing at and ridiculing them for their skimpy skirts and suggestive blouses. I stopped, stepped in front of the pretty blonde cheerleading gal-pals, and told them to "back off and leave the sisters alone or else."

At that moment one of the sisters grabbed a wooden bowling pin left out of the equipment room and tossed it at me. I ducked as it whizzed by my face. Shannon Sharpe then turned to me and said, "You fucking bitch, get out of our business. We don't need your sympathy or your *help*."

Confused, I wondered, *Why wouldn't they want me to defend them? Why were they disgusted with me because I cared about them, and why did they hate me because I stuck up for them?* My feelings of defending the weak and vulnerable hung over me like a soaked emotion that wouldn't dry out. Was I born with a sentimental heart? I hated sentimentalism and never wanted to be seen as weak. Why, then, the compulsion to protect the weak?

## Beginning to Create the Painting—A Piece of White Velvet

I grew up exclusively with White Lutherans and had no experience of what prejudiced behavior looked like toward anyone but poor Whites. At St. Cloud State (SCS), a small state college in upstate Minnesota, I had my first taste of diversity and became friends with some African Americans, guys who came from private high schools and were comfortable mixing with Whites. I thought, *Wow, are these guys ever cool!*

I knew some girls from Shoemaker dorm who signed a pact to date only Black men, and although fear stopped me from signing on, I admired those girls' adventuresome spirit. These African American guy friends nurtured my passion for people different from me and boosted my confidence as someone who can relate to "the oppressed Other." My diversity experience ended when my SDS (Students for a Democratic Society) politics and desire for celebrity status resulted in my expulsion from SCS.

I retreated to my parents' new home in southern Illinois. At Southern Illinois University (SIU) I received an athletic scholarship to play basketball and softball. Although I loved athletics and the experience of being on a team, the conservative leanings of female athletes and my preference for outrageous behavior made my life a topic of conversation. I distanced myself from these "naïve" women and instead discovered men from the English department who were protégés of Jack Kerouac and freeloaders of New York City salons.

Under the influence of these men I honed my coolness, and with their encouragement, I "freed myself" to sleep with Men of Color—my first choice was an Olympian on the Jamaican volleyball team. These Kerouac disciples embraced me as one of their own, and I learned the proud rhetoric of being different. However, they taught me nothing about my racist positioning of coolness or my eroticizing of people of color.

## Stretching the Velvet Over 7 mm Board

By the time I graduated from SIU in the early '70s I was no longer my mother's daughter. The idea of ever living in Richfield or any other suburb seemed counter to my evolved skin. What fueled my politics and righteousness was my disdain for the rich, the sophisticated, and the elite—all synonymous with classism and racism in my mind.

The convergence of the peace movement, the feminist movement, and the civil rights movement gave me the intellectual footing, confidence, and courage to help others. At that time I believed that most Whites were not like me. My belief about my uniqueness and special calling fueled my desire to feel and intervene in "The Other's" pain. I was in a phase of intellectual rapture and set a course to change people's beliefs and convert them to a perspective of knowing based on the way *I* thought about racism and sexism.

## Laying Down the Base Coat With an Airbrush

Throughout my burgeoning anti-racist work in the early '80s, my inflated self-confidence blinded me to how others saw me. I worked as a volunteer in a children's shelter once a month, I ate at restaurants in the "ghetto," I danced in clubs that were predominantly Black, and I sat on the multicultural work committee at school. I spoke out and advocated for children of color whenever there was a sliver of an opening to speak. An obvious omission in my life was women of color. Even though I had no close friends of color I mistakenly thought I understood people of color. I saw the world not as it was but as I was, and my (mis)perception protected me from my ignorance.

I recognized that there were no women of color in my life, and I tried to change that situation. I went out of my way to compliment the Black female teachers I encountered in school. "You have great hair. How did you get it to curl like that—did it take you very long? Your clothing is so cool, where do you shop? You always look so good, girl." Little did I know those women saw me as one more woman of privilege who spoke with unabashed arrogance.

The fact that Black women didn't reciprocate never struck me as odd; I assumed they were caught off guard by my directness. My thick layer of self-confidence continued to protect me from myself. What I did notice, though, was a smirk on the faces of certain Black women as I made my appearance and exited from their circles. Because I believed I was living out my values I assumed they "incorrectly" thought I was like *those other White women.* What Black women did not know about me is that I would fight for them, even if they didn't like me, just like I did for the Sharpe girls.

## Using Masks for Creating Picture Basics

I remained a race-warrior throughout my K–12 teaching career. In 1980 I took a social studies teaching position in an urban school, Lake City High School. In 1980 Lake City's population was 40 percent students of color and 60 percent White, and by 1990 it was 60 percent students of color and 40 percent White. I remained at Lake City until 1990 and then, wanting to make a "bigger" difference, transferred to a Teaching Learning Center (TLC) where I worked with nontraditional students: poor Whites and minority students.

At that time I felt my motives were misjudged, especially by African American parents, and interpreted as hootenanny liberal politics instead of sincere concern. I knew that my desire for justice came from deep inside me. I continued to be hungry for insight into issues of race and racism. In 1995 I entered a graduate program at St. Augustus University (SAU) to pursue a doctorate in educational leadership.

SAU aggressively recruited people of color, and our cohort ended up with seven people of color, four of whom were women. During the first year of SAU's leadership program students heard and embraced each other's stories through faculty-structured immersion activities. It delighted me that one of the Black women, Sondra, seemed genuinely interested in me. I believed (with a skewed understanding) that because Sondra was brilliant—articulate and academically above us all—she could accept me as a peer. I believed I finally found my female friend of color.

## Laying Out the Precut Images

Teaching at the TLC provided a laboratory of multicultural experiences with underserved students and recent immigrant refugees. The sentimental child in me who wanted to help others saw her sweet velvet clown in the faces of my students. TLC was not only a place of diversity but a place where I thrived at teaching while experiencing students' joy at learning, some for the first time.

In our graduate classes, when the conversation turned to race and urban schools, I could call on my experiences at the TLC. I spoke with pride about my efforts to change the wave of prejudiced attitudes by White teachers toward support of students. When issues concerning adults of color were raised I could relate and would detail the emotional/intellectual experiences people of color must be going through. I empathized with the teachers of color and understood their frustrations regarding the insensitivity of the White teachers.

By my third year in graduate school I saw myself as one of the anti-racism leaders of the cohort and someone with the ability to see and accept differences. At TLC several students of color grew to trust me and turned to me for advice. In my history class Carlos, a dark, floppy-haired 18-year-old Latino boy who had a look in his eyes that would melt a glacier, would stay after school and ask for advice. What should he do about his parents' insistence that he go to a trade school? How can he continue in school when he needed money and wanted a job? But his worst fear was how he could escape the trap being set by his girlfriend and her parents' insistence on marriage. Carlos told me he was filled with anxiety because he felt certain his girlfriend, Belle, would end up pregnant. I responded, "Don't you have something to say about that?"

He said, "I know, but her mother expects us to marry since we are sleeping together, and she's pressuring Belle, who's pressuring me to marry her." I wanted him to succeed. I blindly assumed he was better off than his peer group because he escaped the trappings of his culture. He was smart, talented, and could distance himself from his girlfriend. Unfortunately, I told him if he was to make it in the world he must lose the world he came from.

And there was LaToya, an overweight African American girl, a big girl with a personality and love of learning that was just as big—and an incest victim. She needed a safe haven, a place where she could think about going to college, feel loved and respected. She would be my protégé. I tutored her, gave her as much feminist rhetoric as I could fit into a day, and helped her write letters for entrance into the finest private schools on the East Coast. My relationship with LaToya was endlessly rewarding: She admired me. She told me she wanted to be like me, not like her mother.

Smithton, a small private women's college out East, accepted LaToya. But the summer after graduation she had a nervous breakdown. I went to the hospital a couple times to visit her, but I couldn't bear seeing the desperation in her face, and I stopped going and ultimately lost contact with her. Without any knowledge of her family I was left to see myself as her sole mentor. I had failed so she had failed.

After 12 years of teaching in two diverse schools and 6 years of graduate school, with a woman of color as a close friend and students who adored me, I was finally a legitimate nonracist. I couldn't quite identify the parameters of nonracism, but I felt I was special, I belonged, and my passion for a desperate clown emblazoned me. And then my world of being an anti-racist caved in on me.


## Applying Jo Sonya's Acrylic Gouache

Our time together as a cohort at SAU was winding down. During one of our last weekends together, our White middle-class Catholic professor decided we should have one more conversation about race. I enthusiastically seized the opportunity to talk about my experiences with people of color. I talked about the realities of racism and my hope for the White teachers at Lake City and the TLC who didn't get it.

With free reign, I expressed it all, especially my gratitude for being allowed membership in a life I wasn't born into. When I finished I looked over at my friend Sondra, expecting some affirmation for my insight and concern for people of color. Instead she stared at me coldly—the look I had seen often from other African American women. But in addition Sondra also seemed hurt, maybe even embarrassed. Why wasn't she aligning herself with me?

Then I noticed the room had become segregated into Black and White doctoral students, and Sondra was standing next to the other African American women. I was actually surprised. Maybe she didn't want her people to know how much she agreed with me. Before that thought finished its journey through my cerebral pathways Sondra turned to the entire class and said, "Judith, those of us in this class, that is, people of color, wish you would never again take it on yourself to speak for African American students or adults. You may not notice, but you are not African American and you silence us when you speak for us. Please, for your own anti-racist growth *don't tell us what we think*."

At that moment I felt completely betrayed, angry, and humiliated. I heard myself saying, "What do you mean? I didn't mean to speak for you; I didn't intend to silence anyone. I don't think you understood me correctly."

No one responded and a very loud silence hung over the class until the professor jumped up and started telling us the details about finishing the end of the semester.

I wanted to cry, run out of the room, and tell Sondra she was a MF bitch who couldn't be trusted. She did not look at me nor I at her. I moved to a seat next to a six-foot-four blonde White male superintendent friend. Bob was one of only a handful of my friends in the cohort because I had alienated most of the members at some time or another with my righteous, condescending diatribes. He of course understood that Sondra was a bitch, "and who the fuck does she think she is anyway?"

It took every nerve ending to hold in the tears welling up in my eyes. As I sat there I heard nothing except my mind and body convulsing with pain. *How could Sondra betray me? She was my friend!* I had worked hard at being her friend, and this is where it got me? After 20 minutes of sitting with a frozen expression of disinterest, I heard the professor call for a break. I ran out of the room, to my car, and left.

Once home I was still in a state of shock. *How could Sondra humiliate me like that? I was on her side. Why wasn't she on mine?* I figured I was wrong for trusting a Black woman. We are just too different from one another. All I wanted to do was stick up for her, help her live through the ugliness of being oppressed.

The next day at the TLC, still reeling from the hurt I felt by Sondra's comment, I ended up in a confrontation with a Black parent who called me a racist. I went looking for sympathy from Randolph, a Black assistant principal at TLC.

I told Randolph about the ungrateful Black mother and said, "Randolph, what do these parents want? Isn't it enough that I have dedicated my life to helping them and their children?" Without an ounce of understanding or sympathy he said, "You poor White angel, you must get so tired of saving all our people," and walked away.

This time period in my life stands out as the pivotal moment when I challenged my dismissal of my own Whiteness and my defense of my stance of elevating people of color to unnatural heights. Sondra played a major role in that shift.

## Finding the Opacity in the Colors

In pain and hurting, frustrated by the coldness from women of color at school, the loss of Sondra, and administrators who were "idiots," I transferred to the Adult Diploma Program for immigrant adults. I felt unappreciated from my past justice work of scratching and clawing, forgiving and excusing, overcompensating and understanding. Overcome with resentment and anger, I knew the adult immigrant refugee population wanted teachers who cared about them, and I wanted to know my caring meant something.

Throwing myself into my Southeast Asian immigrant students—Vietnamese, Cambodian, Hmong—I felt rejuvenated. I was their hero and they treated me as such. I was tall, they were short; I was funny and they laughed. I spoke about oppression and they agreed with most everything I said. I was the equity-justice advocate as I originally envisioned myself. I taught American history, and the classes flew by, each student excited to be in class, each student showing progress. I thought, *Now* this *is teaching.*

Still, doubts about what was really going on in class lingered. Suspicions gnawed at my elation. Why couldn't I just accept that I was doing some excellent teaching? It appeared that my students were putting me on a pedestal and I couldn't get down. I experienced a growing skepticism about seeing myself as so unique and wonderful. How does one make sense out of a life that moved from "disgraced White" to "teacher extraordinaire"?

## Building Up the Layers of Color Using Wide Flat Brushes With a Rounded Tip

Adding to my discomfort were the voices of my coworkers, who said such things as, "The Hmong people have such a passive, gentle side," "The Vietnamese—how dedicated they are to education . . . ," "The Cambodians are so generous; Americans could learn something from them and how they take care of their elders . . . ," and "The self-control of the Asians in general, why would I ever want to teach anybody else?"

Conversely there were many negative comments about African American adults and their perceived lack of interest in education.

The Hmong are a strong people and learned how to survive race genocide in three countries—but not by being passive and gentle. The Cambodians cared for their people with the ferocity of a culture who had lost three million citizens to the genocide of the Khmer Rouge—not because of some innate value about giving. Vietnamese valued education because of what the French taught them during the colonization of Vietnam, which left many Vietnamese with nothing.

As I grew in knowledge of my students' history as different from my own Euro-American history, I learned that what was perceived as "compliance" was actually grit and determination to succeed. I saw that the hierarchal position of teacher was one of honor, not based on individual skill or teaching practice.

What is this thing called racism? Everyone I worked with was spending many hours beyond their scheduled class time to ensure their Asian students' success. African American adults dropped out of our program while more immigrant refugees transferred in. Without speaking a word about the American Dream, we all had signed on to deliver it to our Asian students. But I felt uncomfortable with what I perceived as my colleagues' over-the-top appreciation of our Asian students.

The Asian refugee/immigrant students were loved by their teachers, and the teachers felt loved by their students. Yet I felt like a fraud. What had I done to deserve this kind of privilege? I wasn't working any harder at this job than the one at TLC. This incongruence and unsettledness left me in a state of disequilibrium.

That experience, coupled with the comments of my colleagues (educated progressive liberals in the finest sense) about Asian students, stranded me on an island, feeling like an outsider in a way different from how I felt after Sondra's comments. Ironically, the continued hum of exaltation and the hymns sung to honor the Asian students set them on a pedestal as well. Here were my colleagues stereotyping the traits and ethnic characteristics of their students. Was this what I did to my African American and Latino students? Wasn't this an inverted racism? I couldn't allow myself to think those thoughts, have self-doubts, see myself as a racist, or question my diversity work. I panicked, thinking I might experience the same humiliation I had with my African American "friends" if I said anything. I thought I'd best keep my mouth shut this time.

## Taking My Time Working From Dark to Light, Leaving Velvet Showing Where I Want Deep Shadows

In 2001 an opportunity ensued to lead a staff development department for North Metro Integration District 21 (NMID 21). I thought this was a chance to make a difference by saving myself, not people of color. I was to lead a collaborative 10-district program; the urban school involved assigned an Afro-centric man to work with my program. This man had routinely used intimidation to "get his way."

Jamal M. Moss was six feet six inches tall, an imposing man who had lots of assumptions about Whites. He believed all White school teachers, except those who aligned with him, were missionary do-gooders. There was some truth to what Jamal said, and quite honestly, his truth didn't bother me as much as his belief that he had an inside track to truth.

Jamal alienated most of the White teachers who were teetering on the edge of wanting to learn more about diversity but scared to death to make a mistake. Those who were outright racist did not care what he said. The people who wanted to be liked by "the Black man" (me, four years earlier) were his disciples.

Fortunately, many of the people of color I worked with did not share his view. Unfortunately, he came to represent "the Black man" in the largest urban district in the metro area and was the spokesperson on diversity to the 10 district White male superintendents. My new learning about my own racism kept me off balance with Jamal, a state Jamal seemed to prefer for Whites.

Watching Jamal work was like watching a conquer-and-destroy mission that divided people into "us" and "them," victim/offender—a familiar strategy I had seen many White people employ. One of the unintended lessons I learned about racial conflict from Jamal is that White people react with stereotype conclusions, and Blacks are looking to counter the intimidation they grew up feeling.

When around Jamal, my German American righteousness and blame-and-shame temper flared, and my anger about racism and prejudice became the anger and fear of hopelessness. Jamal was charged with ensuring the practices in schools did not discriminate against children of color. But his relationship with people who disagreed with him made it difficult for a teacher to challenge him and his ideas. Not all teachers were angered by Jamal; many wanted his approval, the stamp of having an anti-racist position. But did they change? Did they want to change their practices or just sing Jamal's songs?

Was Jamal's self-serving, counterproductive approach that different from those of other diversity workers, including mine? What had the diversity industry done the past 25 years to change the lives of children of color? Who were these people in the diversity business, and why were they making so little difference in the education of students of color? After all, in the last 25 years the achievement gap had only grown.

I needed to look no further than at my own life. I had dedicated my educational pursuit to justice and equality for all children. Had I been as ineffective as Jamal? What had my body of work really meant in terms of change and progress for parents and children of color in public schools? What I learned from Jamal brought me to another landmark in my journey. Once again I felt very uncomfortable with my beliefs and approaches. This time I had nowhere to run. I knew I needed to journey deeper into my worldview to understand the picture of effective cross-cultural work—the hues, the form, the special qualities, the depth, and the smell of change—in order to elevate my work.

## Cleaning the Surface With a Lint Brush As I Work

This dissonance and uncomfortable sense of being wrong about what I had been so sure about took me on a journey back to the velvet clown and childhood empathy. As a child I cared deeply about others' pain and saw no righteousness in that. At the age of 12 I couldn't understand others' points of view, but what 12-year-old can? Now I knew I could take that vulnerable empathy and match it with understanding. I had to think like the Sharpes, understand Sondra's anger at my comments, and wonder what LaToya's mother and Carlos's family thought of my relationship with their child.

The job of the culturally sensitive human being is to appreciate the other's experience from where he or she is positioned, not from my own privileged position.

Like most learning acquired from immersion in one's own life, my excellent mistakes taught me how to live in a diverse world, and as I detailed them for this piece I wondered, *How can I say out loud these humiliating experiences? What will happen to my diversity contracts?* I know now that what I embraced was learning and that my failures taught me to be more interculturally sensitive and . . . *What diversity contracts?*

It was crucial to make excellent mistakes; it was vital to know at the level of humiliation that I had misunderstood my reliance on stereotypes, mistaken my arrogance as confidence, and relied on my White privilege in my service to people of color. But what served me in the end was a desire for justice. Even if it was blinded by my Whiteness, the love of a velvet clown seeped through.

## Understanding That Acrylic Velvet Is Very Forgiving and Durable

Thus began a series of reflections. I started to flip through the past scenarios in my life. I realized when I stopped trying to sculpt a life of anti-racism I liked living an integrated life of differences. I lived a life that was diverse and interactive with many people unlike me. I knew it and felt the richness of difference, but it was no longer the anti-racist hero's image I had somehow been trapped in.

When choosing White friends I felt more comfortable in the presence of unusual types, oddballs—odd and suspect. Having creative types as friends wasn't a result of seeking out people on the fringe; it was simply wanting a life that was interesting. My curiosity and need for a fuller life— going beyond an Anglo ethnocentric perspective—originally gave me the courage to mount an intentional journey of diversity. When one has an obsession to be with others different from oneself and a curiosity to see the world as something to discover, the beauty is that anyone—even I—can be interculturally sensitive.

The difference for me was to think of myself as a diverse person instead of an expert in diversity. When I look back at my life I know I fumbled along, afraid to tell anyone what I was really feeling. My silence left me a loner, slithering along a slimy, wet, and cold path that needed a false sense of self to attempt the work. That changed at NMID 21 because the leadership team, people of color and White educators, knew we all needed to understand each other better and could do that by standing by each other as we each made ignorant assumptions about "The Other" that weren't true.

It was predictable how the work in some ways became simpler when I no longer needed to be the expert. I moved from the altruistic, benevolent service worker to simply a person who wants to understand why people think what they think.

## Hanging My Clown in My Cityscape House

At NMID 21 we were a small group of diverse folks who wanted most to make a difference. We all had a misunderstood clown in our closet. I became very close to all three women on the team but especially close to one of the Black women working in an all-White district.

Like other friendships, ours was both unique and mundane. It was based on our individuality and our mutual attraction. When we were with each other we could be vulnerable; we did not have to protect ourselves from the deep wounds of racial hurt. In other words, we let ourselves excuse our ignorance about each other in order to have a close and vulnerable friendship.

My participation in our interactions as someone developing a friendship with a colleague changed the dynamic between us. She was not the ethnographic experience of diversity for me as other Black women had been in the past. Her ability to see me as a unique person, something she appreciated in all her friends, freed me from the need to be hyper-vigilant about race. I did not feel she was watching to see if I would make a wrong move. I no longer believed I had to perform for her. The paradigm shift from expert to friend was a shift from researcher to person, from missionary to loved one, from caretaker to cherished one.

The canvas on which all my cross-racial experiences are now painted is real friendship. Behind this learning are images of me—me thinking that if I dated or slept with a person of color I had an inside track on being anti-racist, me using stereotypes as an aid to becoming friends with the women of color at Lake City School, me assuming I could approach Asian adults with little regard for their history, me speaking for my African American colleagues in my graduate school program, me never once thinking I should call my students' parents, assuming I knew what was best for their child—these are the images I remember in order to stay humble.

Intentionally integrating my life is a way to achieve an anti-racist perspective. The route to an anti-racist life is unnerving, unkempt, littered with messy relationships. If it were a work of art it would be a velvet clown painting, a fabric of divergent colors, textures, and depth—a narrative with sentiment, brokenness, and a need for a community.

## Journal Questions

1. In flow writing, journal the "learnings" you bring to your work from your upbringing and family (see "Journaling" in the introduction of this book for a description of flow writing). Have you found yourself stuck in any of them? Which ones keep you going in spite of obstacles?

2. Journal about a setting in which you felt safe to share your "excellent mistakes" working with children. In which were you unsafe? What components were there to help or hinder its feeling safe?

3. Write about growing up in a "post–civil rights" era. Does race matter as much as in the past or not? Do you feel a big distance between you and your students because of race? What sensibilities do your students have about their race?

*Kathleen Tindle*

3

# LOOK FOR CONNECTIONS— THEY ARE THERE ADRIFT

*Kathleen Tindle*

"I got to see demanding work that often took my breath away when I witnessed my preservice teachers grappling with the realities of racism that limited or locked their students out of access to power and persisting in their attempts to right the wrongs and support their students' learning, voice, and power."

B orn into a military family in 1958, I was the fourth and youngest girl of what would eventually be five children, bookend brothers with three girls in the middle. I began life having to move every three years. I learned how to observe my surroundings to adapt and fit in quickly. It wasn't easy to fit in because I had only one parent, my dad, after the spring of 1965, when my mom died of colon cancer.

Death made our family different, and our family dynamic changed in many ways. In 1966, when my dad was transferred to England, my eldest brother stayed behind to finish his high school years and the four youngest went off to England, away from the rest of our family and all our friends.

My dad was emotionally unavailable but was doing the best he could given the situation. Our family was adrift, each one of us figuring out how to get through our emotional trauma. Many adults on the air force base in England pitied us; some moms reached out with casseroles or pies and strange smiles with sad eyes. I hated that people felt that we were different and treated us with pity. It made me angry and ashamed.

It was my third-grade teacher that year who made me want to become a teacher. Each Friday she would play her guitar and sing to us. I loved how calm I would feel when she played and loved how that music made me feel part of a community. I felt loved and cherished by my teacher, and I wanted to make others feel that same way. That is what teaching was, and remains, for me—a vehicle to build community, to come together and get through tough times in productive, caring ways.

## White Meets Black

By 1969 my dad retired from the air force, and we settled back into the house in Prince George's (PG) County, Maryland, where we were living when our mom died. PG County is a suburb of Washington, DC, and at the time 55 percent of PG County's population was African American, with most White and Black residents in a similar socioeconomic bracket. However, the neighborhoods were segregated. Even after the *Brown v. Board of Education* decision in 1954, the Prince George's County Public School System (PGCPS) was slow to change its segregated schools. In 1964 the Department of Health, Education, and Welfare (HEW) got involved, and in 1971 it found PGCPS noncompliant. A court case brought by a group of African American parents found that PGCPS was illegally segregating Blacks and required it to implement a desegregation plan by January 1973. To achieve desegregation, the school system decided to bus students from neighborhood to neighborhood to attend schools across the county.

I attended seventh and eighth grades in a PGCPS junior high school from 1970 to 1972. It was a tumultuous time in PGCPS history, but my school was somewhat segregated and majority White. However, at the end of my eighth-grade year it was announced that many Black students would be attending different schools in the following year because of the busing plan. The Black students were upset, and during the last two or three days of school there were incidents of violence.

One morning I was standing at my locker to organize my books for my morning classes. I was concentrating on collecting my materials when someone threw the raw egg that broke on top of the lockers near mine. It didn't splash on me, but it was dripping down the nearby lockers. I thought, *how gross*, then ignored it and continued to rummage in my locker. When I closed the locker door with my books held close to my chest and turned to leave for class, the hallway was blocked by Black students.

I was shocked. I was scared. My heart was beating so fast! The egg had been used to identify a White victim—me—for physical violence. My first thought was, *When they start to hit me it's going to really hurt because I'm going to be pushed against all these locker handles.*

Without really thinking about it, I started to push through the crowd as if they were not there to harm me. I mumbled "Excuse me," kept my head down, and just pushed my way through. When they realized that I was walking freely down the hallway they surrounded me again. Now I was against the wall and a semi-circle of Black students was surrounding me. As I kept my books clutched to my chest for protection, I vainly searched for a familiar face but found none. A girl stepped in front of me and said, "You know, if someone hits you, you should hit them back." My eyes got huge and my heart beat even faster. I meekly said, "No one is going to hit anyone," and I turned, pushed my way forcefully through some students, and began to run toward the office. A few students pulled my hair as I went by, but they all scattered through the halls, seeing that I was heading toward the office.

I ran to the office and waited for the assistant principal to be available to talk with me. Now that I had a few minutes to sit quietly, I began to think about the possibility of being physically hurt and started to feel scared and shake a little. After I reported the event my morning continued without incident.

The next time students were allowed to go to their lockers was after lunch. Toward the end of lunch my heart started beating faster as I began to get scared about returning to my locker, fearing that the same mob of students would try again to target me. I asked the assistant principal to walk me to my locker. He wouldn't escort me, but he did walk a little ways behind me, and his presence calmed my nerves. The few remaining days of the school year passed without further incidents or threats of violence.

As a 13-year-old I didn't understand (and still don't understand) how violence could be a useful solution to anger, but I was able to empathize with the feelings of being treated as different and with condescension, and of being disregarded, coming out of the system's decision to compel Black students to go to schools foreign to them across town. I had never fit in at any of my schools, never had attended any school long enough to feel a part of things. I grew up without my mom and had to handle emotional trauma at an early age. So I understood the students' anger even then and didn't blame them. I was also able to recognize that the random selection by the thrown egg meant that it was not about me.

However, my dad and his new wife were not so sympathetic, and during the summer of 1972 our family moved outside of Annapolis, Maryland. I started high school in Anne Arundel County Public Schools. As an adult I realize that my family had been able to move away because we had the means to do so. Although my family comes from strong "blue collar" roots (my dad hung wallpaper, pumped gasoline, and was drafted twice before staying in the military) and we didn't have much money at all, we still had more money than many of the African American families living nearby.

I know now that we lived in a house that was considered expensive. The Black kids nicknamed our street "Peanut Butter Hill." They said that after buying a house on this street, all you could afford to eat was peanut butter. I also recall the groups of Black students walking past our house after getting off the school bus, to get to their own neighborhoods, which were situated past a broken fence at the end of the street. I didn't recognize these obvious economic disparities, and the power that our socioeconomic level gave my family, until I was an adult.

## Acceptance and Welcome

I attended University of Wisconsin at Milwaukee from 1979 to 1981, finishing my bachelor of science in urban elementary and science education. I was ready to help kids learn and to make them feel comforted and cared for when they were with me.

The Milwaukee Public Schools system was under court order to desegregate its schools from 1976 to 1979. Historically, African Americans had settled in Milwaukee's city center after World War II, creating all-Black neighborhoods and therefore all-Black neighborhood schools. The court order in the late 1970s mandated integration through busing, which involved 75 percent of the students in the Milwaukee system. It also created specialty schools with magnet programs. In 1981, through my student teaching in Milwaukee elementary schools, I came into direct contact with schools affected by this court order and with the Black community in the public schools. My first authentic interaction and relationship building within the Black community was through the Milwaukee teachers.

I was accepted—with reservation—by the Milwaukee teachers. I first had to demonstrate my skills and dispositions about teaching Black students so that the teachers could see if my actions matched my rhetoric. Once I had created lessons that considered the students' backgrounds and that the students had responded to with enthusiasm, then the teachers accepted me as a White teacher who truly cared about the students, did not view them from a disposition of pity, and didn't consider myself to be "saving" them from their "downtrodden" lives.

Because of my earlier experiences of being treated as "less than" when I was a child, I did not see the students as having deficits but rather recognized that they already had skills and believed my job was to help build on these skills. I created a social studies unit for first-grade students on "Community," and together we built a model community of cardboard boxes that the students designed. It included some small houses but mostly apartment buildings and corner stores—just like their own community.

In a science lesson on static electricity with sixth-grade students, I had not foreseen an obvious complication. The method I planned to use to demonstrate static electricity was to rub a balloon on the students' heads and then pull the balloon away so the students could see and feel their hair being pulled by the static electricity created from the friction. Of course this didn't work, because of the hair products Blacks use on their hair, and my students had a good laugh at/with me about it—especially when all the students had to gather around and rub their balloons on my hair for the experiment. But the students enjoyed messing up my hair and being able to teach me something. The Milwaukee teachers, while enjoying my faux pas, also appreciated my approach to correcting the error when I acknowledged to the students that I had a lot to learn from them.

At the end of my student teaching the Milwaukee teachers took me out to lunch at a local Black family-owned restaurant. This was my first taste of "soul food," and it was delicious. We ate a meal of fried chicken, collard greens, corn bread, mashed potatoes, and sweet tea. The afternoon is memorable for me because I had such a rush of emotions. This warm community of caring Black teachers was willing to accept me, in these tense political times, with all my shortcomings and differences as a White female novice teacher in a predominantly Black school system, and they did so without pity or condescension. Acceptance and welcome are two of the most marvelous feelings in the human condition, something I had missed growing up without a mom. I was never more happy about or sure of my decision to work with high-needs students in urban areas than I was at that lunch in 1981.

## Becoming Culturally Responsive

By 1985 I was living in a predominantly African American neighborhood near the "Eighth and H Street Crew" in northeast Washington, DC, and teaching seventh-grade students in a community 30 minutes south of DC. The middle school's community was racially mixed, but the White families enjoyed a higher socioeconomic status compared to most of the Black families living in the subsidized housing across the street from the school.

The faculty at the school somewhat mirrored its community's racial mix, but not that of the students. There were many more White teachers (about 80 percent) than Black teachers (about 20 percent), but the student population was closer to 60 percent White and 40 percent Black. The principal was a White male, and the assistant principal, Doris, was a Black female who was formerly a social studies teacher at the school. Doris and I had taught on the same seventh-grade team before she became an administrator, so we had become friendly as we worked together to deliver instruction to the same group of students.

After a year of teaching at the middle school I had made some observations of the racial divide and power structures in the school community and within the school itself. In the school community there was a separation between the White and Black families. The Black families generally lived in the subsidized section of housing in walking distance from the school. The White families lived farther away, so White children took the school bus or were driven by parents to school. This distinction in housing screamed out the differences in socioeconomic level of the families in the community, creating a stressor in relationships among the students. This was also a time of racial transition in the community as many Black families moved there, developing what are now pockets of "majority minority" neighborhoods.

The influx of Black families into majority White communities created racial tension, and White families responded by moving to more affluent areas in the county where Black families could not afford to live. I would often reflect on these observations as I drove my 30-minute commute to and from my Black neighborhood in DC.

In the school many White teachers expected Black students to perform poorly academically because they interpreted the families' behavior of not attending school meetings or being difficult to communicate with about school matters to mean that the families did not care about education. More Black students were assigned to special education and referred to the office for discipline reasons than were White students. Most surprising to me, however, was the lack of interactions between the White and Black faculty. They did not eat together during lunch, sat in generally separate groups during faculty meetings, and did not socialize together after school. Black teachers didn't even park in the same area of the teacher parking lot as the White teachers but instead clustered their cars in a row at the back of the lot.

I knew from conversations with my White colleagues that they either were unwilling to admit there was a conscious division or were okay with the division. I felt compelled to address this tension among the faculty with my Black colleagues to assuage any thoughts they may have had about my acceptance of or complicity in this divide. I wanted my Black colleagues to know about my beliefs and dispositions, to know of my anti-racist stance and my desire to teach all students through collaborative means with all of my colleagues.

I penned a petition to the "African American Community" of the school requesting that I be considered an "honorary member" of the Community and thenceforth be considered "African American." In my petition, as an attempt at humor, I outlined details about my life with exaggerated stereotypes about African Americans that would indicate I could be considered Black: I lived in a Black neighborhood within a predominantly Black city; I listened to jazz growing up, when my father played his trumpet along with "Satchmo" on the record player; I ate soul food, and watermelon was my favorite fruit; and I knew biographies of powerful and influential Black scientists. I told the imaginary committee that, if accepted, I would park my car in the back of the lot where they parked their cars. My petition also acknowledged, on a serious note, that I had a lot to learn about being Black and that the reason I wanted to be an honorary member was that I wanted to teach my Black students well so they could excel. I wanted to reach my students and needed guidance and support from my Black colleagues to reach this goal. I turned in my petition to Doris and waited for a response.

At the end of a faculty meeting Doris asked me to stay behind to talk. As the faculty streamed out of the auditorium I went down toward the front where Doris waited for me. She was gathering her things together and making small talk. When she looked up from her papers she had me turn toward the seats, and gathered there were most of the Black teachers and staff in the school. Doris told me that they had considered my petition and had decided to make me an honorary member of the Community.

Doris shook my hand as if it were an official ceremony, and then others came forward too. Some of my colleagues had prepared ideas for me about becoming a more authentic Community member by getting past stereotypes and getting to know people at a personal level. I knew then that using the exaggerated stereotypes in my attempt at humor to acknowledge and bridge the racial divisions had hit a raw nerve with some of my colleagues and that I would have to work very hard to become a worthy member of the Community. The ceremony ended with laughing and hugging and completely turned around my teenage experience of being surrounded by egg-carrying angry Black students.

## Life's Purpose

The separation between the White and Black communities in this school system continued, as did the achievement gap. I continued to formally study culturally responsive methodologies along with the science content in my master's degree program. As department chair and team leader, I attempted to work with my veteran colleagues to reach *all students* by advocating the creation of strong relationships with students and their families and the use of students' own backgrounds and interests to create lessons that included aspects of their culture.

The idea of changing teaching practices to better meet all students' learning potential was not usually welcomed by my White colleagues, and I often found myself disillusioned and lost. These veteran teachers seemed more interested in crafting their lessons for students from White middle-class families and did not see it as their mission to facilitate Black students' learning, which they deemed to be operating at a "lower" level. These teachers believed that students who struggled with learning only struggled because they didn't work hard enough or care enough about their own education, and that it was up to someone else to address these poor study habits or attitudes. Of course, most of the struggling students were students of color, and these teachers were using these rationalizations to hide their racist views and practices.

I found fewer obstacles to the notion of teaching all students when I collaborated with and mentored new teachers, fresh from the university, who held dispositions similar to my own about a teacher's role and responsibilities to meet all students' needs. When the opportunity arose to form completely new teams of teachers, I was able to help establish a team of seventh-grade teachers, all White, ready and willing to address every student's learning needs by using and building from their strengths.

I had been teaching for more than 10 years, but each of the other team members had taught fewer than 6. We taught together for two years without disruption to our team. We worked many long hours in collaborative team planning sessions to create thematic units across the four content areas (English, math, science, and social studies), and virtually every day our team discussed what our individual students were learning, what they still needed to learn, and how to better reach them. Many families requested that their child be placed on our team, and occasionally the administration requested that we take on and work with a struggling seventh-grade student well-known for behavioral or learning difficulties. We were proud of our students' response to our work and dedication, and the response of the students' families.

Working with this team of like-minded teachers for those two years was invigorating and inspiring. It forced me to acknowledge the difference between teachers unwilling to change because of their own biases and prejudices, limiting their view of a teacher's role and responsibilities, and those teachers who frame the educational process through social justice. I began to wonder about how to get teachers to see education through this lens and thereby embrace culturally responsive pedagogies. I took a leave of absence to formally study these notions through a doctoral program at George Washington University. On graduating in 2000, I was asked by the university to direct an urban teacher preparation program that framed its curriculum in social justice, and that is what I did for 13 years.

My work involved preparing graduate students, recruited for their predisposition to and experiences in social justice, to teach all students in high-needs school settings in which most of the students come from families living in generational cycles of poverty. I got to see demanding work that often took my breath away when I witnessed my preservice teachers grappling with the realities of racism that limited or locked their students out of access to power and persisting in their attempts to right the wrongs and support their students' learning, voice, and power.

## The Learning Continues

As I work with preservice teachers invested in framing education as social justice, I found that I continued to learn and grow in the area of race relations and cultural sensitivity. I continued to make assumptions that were incorrect, but on reflection I altered my views to accommodate a more authentic and contextual version of reality. The two examples that follow involve two different female Black graduate students who were in my urban teacher preparation project.

Justine was from a middle-class family and grew up in the Southwest. Her application was strong, and she scored high in her interview protocol around issues of social justice. My assumption was that because she was Black she would be a great asset to her fellow White cohort members as an "ambassador" of sorts into the world of Black culture. I further assumed that she would be a welcomed role model by the Black students at the high school. However, Justine's middle-class status held a stronger influence over her than did her connections to high-poverty Black urban youth. She struggled to balance her belief that all students deserve a quality education with her interpretation of student behaviors as "lazy" or "unmotivated." I found that I had to work harder with Justine than with the White preservice teachers to get her to reflect deeply about knowing her students well enough to interpret their behavior within a context instead of judging their behaviors against her own value system. Being Black is not in and of itself an automatic connection between teachers and students. Socioeconomic background also figures prominently.

Another Black preservice teacher, Deirdre, was from a similar socioeconomic background as the high school students. She was from the West Coast and was one of the first to attend college in her family. After about four months at the high school Deirdre began to exhibit frustration and anger toward the veteran teachers at the school, the Black teachers in particular. I was unsure what might be causing this, and my first thought was that Deirdre was overwhelmed by all the graduate work required of her on top of her teaching full-time every day at the high school. However, when I checked in with her we had a discussion about something very different.

Deirdre was very upset because she interpreted the poor teaching she had observed by Black veteran teachers to be evidence of social injustice, all the more egregious because the poor teaching was being done by Black teachers to Black students. She felt let down by her own race and disgraced that her own people could perpetuate the racist systems often inherent in poor-quality school districts. Again, I had to be reminded by my Black student about the pride of the Black culture and how that is such an important piece to always consider in any context.

The learning continues and my investment grows deeper and stronger. I feel I have come full circle, from my early days of experiencing the feelings of being "Other" and being adrift to having a mission and vision that feeds my soul and gives my life purpose.

## Journal Questions

1. Journal about your middle school experience: Was race an issue? What's the most memorable experience you had in middle school that was informed by poverty, racism, or other isms? Did you ever have an egg thrown at your locker?

2. In your journal describe the "Peanut Butter Hill" you grew up in or didn't grow up in. Reflect on the feelings you have as you think back to your childhood home, and include them in your journal piece.

3. In your journal, using your own school as a reference point, defend or disagree with the following statement: "In the school many White teachers expected Black students to perform poorly academically because they interpreted the families' behavior of not attending school meetings or being difficult to communicate with about school matters to mean that the families did not care about education."

4. In your journal write a letter to a White faculty member at your school requesting honorary membership into their race group, using stereotypes that define their group and that you believe you could and would uphold in order to secure membership.

*Kat Griffith*

4

# OF PRIVILEGE, APPROVAL, AND A SAVIOR COMPLEX

*Kat Griffith*

"I have to be willing to completely remake myself as a teacher. I have to accept that my privileged world has in some respects unsuited me to teach these children, and that part of giving up my privilege may mean giving up my freedom to be any kind of teacher I like. I need to be what they need, whatever that is."

You could say that my journey as an educator started when, at 12 years old, I found a copy of Jonathan Kozol's *Death at an Early Age* lying on a coffee table. The book—about the appalling schools of African American children in Boston—set me on fire. During the next few years, I followed Kozol around like a puppy dog whenever he spoke somewhere. I also remember buying a copy of Judge Garrity's legal decision to desegregate Boston's schools. It had a map illustrating Boston's school districting lines, snaking around to lasso in or exclude individual apartment buildings.

During my high school years, I devoured like an addict an entire genre of books in the Kozol mold: heroic teachers (usually White) teaching in inner-city schools (usually Black). They wrote with vivid passion of the outrages their students experienced, and how they had inspired even the most hardened young cynics in their classrooms. I once gave a book report in my ninth-grade English class in which I presented eight of these books at once. I also did an independent study on alternative education that took me to alternative schools all over Boston. To my bitter disappointment, I didn't meet any other real-life Kozols, and my life moved on in other directions.

During the next 30 years, I lived, worked, and traveled for seven years in Latin America; I earned a master's degree in agricultural economics; I got married, had two children, and settled in Wisconsin; and I finally began my teaching career—as a homeschooler.

I will confess that, even at my happiest teaching Spanish, economics, writing, and Great Books to groups of homeschoolers, I had moments of introspection over the fact that I was lavishing all my energy and first-rate education on very few kids—kids who were going to do fine with or without me. I did not feel I was furthering social justice or living the dream I'd had.

## Revelations

In winter 2002 I attend a five-day workshop with Niyonu Spann: Beyond Diversity 101. It is unlike any workshop I have ever attended. I don't learn about race per se, but I learn about the "me" that intersects with the issue of race. Two revelations: First, I am, to the core, a rich kid. This emerges during an exercise of grouping ourselves by the social class in which we were raised (working class, middle class, privileged). I hover physically between middle class and privileged, not wanting to claim privilege but not really relating to what the middle-class people are saying. When the small privileged group finally speaks, I recognize myself immediately.

What I learn is that my privilege consists less in money than in overall security and an unshakeable sense of entitlement to a place at the table. I expect to be heard and taken seriously. I expect to walk into any public institution and get a respectful hearing. On the rare occasions when I'm treated unfairly I'm able to mount a polite but robust defense. This knowledge of how to work with people in authority, this confidence in my own efficacy, and the fact that people with power and privilege recognize me as one of their own and treat me accordingly has been and is a defining feature of my life.

My privilege hits me over the head at the workshop as a sudden and painful revelation. I describe it at the time as "coming out as a rich kid." It ends a lifetime of convenient personal lies that have twisted and distorted my behavior for years around issues of money and power and—often—race. I realize that my denials of my privilege have made me blind to others' oppression, and that my denials of my own power have in no way empowered others.

The second revelation of the workshop is that I am utterly dependent on approval from those in power for my sense of well-being. I experience a first: approval deprivation at a workshop. How is it that for once I seem not to have convinced the facilitator that I am special? If I am not special I am nobody! This actually shatters me to such a degree that I almost have to leave the workshop.

Initially I believe this need for approval is purely an outgrowth of family-of-origin dynamics, and in important ways it is. However, in hindsight, I also see that my social privilege has played a role in maintaining this dependence. I have never had to develop the strength to stand on my own against a loss of approval, because I can count on it. It's easy not to know you're addicted to something if it comes to you constantly.

As I wrestle over the next couple of years with this issue of my addiction to approval, I realize that it is intimately linked with my decision to homeschool rather than teach in a public school. I realize that my psychological reality has unfitted me to do the social justice work that I believe needs to be done, and that I am increasingly discerning in what I'm being called to do. I come to see that not to grapple with this is to render myself impotent to do the work that is mine to do.

## Of Ignorance and Education

Something in me knows this: I won't be able to handle a classroom of angry, turned-off, troubled kids, because why on earth would they approve of some do-gooder White woman with a savior complex? Some part of me knows that I'll be crucified. So I have retreated into a safe world of gentle hippies and Christian homeschoolers and lovely, easy children.

But I feel a nudge to start moving. So I decide to teach a course on the civil rights movement. Almost from the first day, I am riveted. And awed. And ashamed. And inspired. And outraged. It jolts me into awareness of a significant feature of my privilege: the privilege to remain ignorant. I realize that nothing I am learning is hard to find out—I have simply made no effort to educate myself about it before, and neither has a single teacher at any level of my privileged, first-class education.

Furthermore, I see that the superficial portrayals of the civil rights movement I have experienced up until this point are a *whitewash*, in every sense of the word. African Americans did almost all the heavy lifting, and relatively few Whites took real risks, paid real costs, or were in it for the long haul.

This, believe it or not, is news to me. I have grown up surrounded by White people who claim the civil rights movement as something of a collective White triumph, something we did for Black people.

I become convinced during the year that I teach this course that I am being called to lay down homeschooling and somehow work for racial justice. I start to experiment. I write a series of feature articles on immigrants in Ripon that is printed in our local paper over 13 weeks. I work with another friend to start a Quaker worship group at a nearby prison. I join a county diversity network, I run for the school board, and I begin working as a Spanish interpreter for the school district. I also start to work on putting my kids in school.

## Privilege Personified

When I contact the schools about enrolling my children, I am met with brick walls, rude administrators, dismissive teachers, endless nonresponses to my calls. . . . It is bewildering.

An acquaintance gives me the phone number of the district psychologist, whose name I recognize from a party several years before. I call her and explain the stonewalling I am experiencing. She tells me exactly who to call and what to ask for, and says to tell them she sent me.

When I refer to the psychologist by her first name as a friend, suddenly the doors fly open. The messages are answered, the calls are returned. Once I get my foot in the door, the reception I receive is everything to which a lifetime of privilege has accustomed me. I even write a letter to the superintendent describing my experience, and he calls a formal meeting to meet with homeschoolers, apologize, and discuss how to make the process smoother.

I eventually find out why I wasn't well received initially. I am enrolling my kids close on the heels of two former homeschooling families whose children have significant behavioral and cognitive problems. The families are also working class, and one of the children is part African American. I see the doors that privilege alone—the "right" friend—opens for me, and what doors close on the presumption that I am working class with needy kids and/or kids of color. Same schools, different worlds.

My next refresher course in privilege comes at the prison where I volunteer. My world celebrates individuality and smiles tolerantly on creative rule bending. The prison introduces me to a world built of walls and rules and rigidity with everything in lockstep.

After a few months at the prison I make a calamitous mistake: I bring a book requested by a prisoner. When the guards find the book, they make an emergency PA announcement of a security breach at the front desk. The deputy warden banishes me from the premises and puts me on the state blacklist for prison visitation, and the prisoner involved is given eight months in solitary confinement. BLAMMO. The offending book? *The Federalist Papers.*

It is the single most humiliating event of my life. I am treated like a despised stupid liberal do-gooder, a chump, a dupe, a dangerous fraternizer, a partner in crime. There is nothing in my life that has prepared me for the hard edges of the prison industrial complex, nothing that has taught me to be careful around this kind of power. The ton-of-bricks reaction to my transgression is completely without precedent in my life.

The day I am kicked out of the prison is also the day I have been invited to a teacher's union meeting with my intent to run for the school board. If elected I will be the only new member of the board, with which the union has been deadlocked in a bitter dispute over contract negotiations. They're hoping I will be on their side. I realize at this meeting that I will not survive the heat in this kitchen, that I would need skin like a rhinoceros or I would need to be Gandhi. Lacking either trait, I withdraw from the race. With my name already on the ballot, I am elected anyway. It feels like a terrible cop out, but I can't summon the strength to withstand the anger and the bitterness and union disapproval that seem inevitable, so I withdraw again.

Over the next few months, I retreat into an emotional cave and lick my wounds. I try to make sense of how my "leadings" could have turned into such a colossal mess. It seems like almost everything I have tried has ended in my doing damage where I had hoped to help. It is a very low point in my life. I feel a strong sense of leading to work for racial and social justice, and I turn out to be both extraordinarily inept and an emotional weakling. I recognize another facet of my privilege: the privilege to back out of a struggle because I'm not enjoying myself. I can walk away, and I have. My failure feels complete.

## Living the Call

I sign up for 10 more days with Niyonu Spann over the summer: a repeat of Beyond Diversity 101 and a subsequent Training for Trainers workshop. Both workshops take me deep into the woods spiritually and emotionally. But what is most important is that I find my key to moving forward.

I identify that shame is paralyzing me, and I learn this: *My shame is exactly as big as my pride.* I come to see that if I can lose the myth of my own perfectibility—the shaky foundation for my pride—I can lose the shame. If I could lose the shame, I'd no longer have to sequester myself from the world to avoid making mistakes and risking a loss of approval. If I could lose the shame, I could dare to try things and dare to make mistakes and look bad and suffer a loss of approval—including from people of color—and I could pick myself up and move on.

Within weeks of figuring this out, I get an urgent call from the high school principal asking me if I'd be willing to teach one section of Spanish 5. I have no certification, not a single education course under my belt, or a degree in Spanish. But I have interpreted many times for the district, and I have prior relationships with many Hispanic immigrants who have moved to our small, rural town of 7,000. I am hired on an emergency license.

Over the next year, even though I am teaching mainly elite Anglo students, I nevertheless get increasingly immersed in the world of our English language learner (ELL) students, getting to know them, tutoring them, advocating for them, and eventually writing a proposal to teach a Heritage Spanish class for native speakers. To my amazement, the board approves the class on the first vote, and it starts in September of 2009.

It is the hardest class I have ever taught, and over the course of a few weeks a painful realization creeps up on me. I realize that I have always experienced my students as being good followers. If I am a good leader, they will follow, and then I can take them pretty much anywhere. These students, however, mill about randomly, occasionally charge around chaotically, and are proceeding slowly despite my nips, nudges, and tireless efforts to keep them focused. This is alarming and discouraging to me. My students and I are hopelessly mismatched.

I struggle to become the teacher I think they need, but she is so at odds with who I think I am. I consult with everyone, I read books on classroom management and instructional strategies, and I watch videos on discipline. I try altering my behaviors to fit theirs, and I feel like a klutz and a fraud. I am not very convincing.

I am also increasingly appalled by the academic level of the kids, their inattention, their disorganization, and their failure to follow through on things. Half of them show up to class without pencils day after day. I try various strategies. I attach big garish flowers to loaner pencils to mark them as mine. I figure my macho boys won't want flowers waving around as they write, but I'm wrong. My classroom looks like a greenhouse some days.

Gradually the flowers are peeled off and my pencils walk out with my students. Next I start demanding a shoe as collateral for a loaner pencil. Pretty soon I have a heap of shoes in the front of the room and I'm tripping over it. One day a kid builds a shoe sculpture, artistically dramatizing the ridiculousness of the situation.

The kids' behavior continues to deteriorate until things are getting ugly. I have moments where the big knot of boys outside my classroom every morning feels a little gangy to me. I have moments in which I find them scary. I wonder guiltily, *Is this just my being racist? Am I just a typical White woman afraid of some big Mexican kid simply because he's not acting cowed and humble? Why am I afraid of these guys, and I'm not afraid of the White wrestlers and football players who also frequent the hall?* I start to hear comments from some of my colleagues in the same hall who are also thinking they feel the gangy vibe.

I have moments of regret that I ever created this course and gave these kids a chance to get together. And I have guilty thoughts about what that says: that I like integration only as long as I'm not in the minority? that I'm scared to let the students of color get together because I might lose control?

I'm horrified that my feelings look like typical racist-White-person feelings. Was I wrong to think I was supposed to do this?

The first two times the principal observes my class he is favorably impressed despite some problems. The third time he is shocked, and he lets me know that it is absolutely essential that I take control. Lucky for me, he is deeply supportive and willing to work with me. But I have a mountain range I have to cross before I can crack down.

## Scaling the Mountain

The first peak: My style of leadership is not, at the moment, working at all. I have to be something else, at least temporarily and maybe forever. I have to be willing to completely remake myself as a teacher. I have to accept that my privileged world has in some respects unsuited me to teach these children, and that part of giving up my privilege may mean giving up my freedom to be any kind of teacher I like. I need to be what they need, whatever that is.

The second peak: My kids do not love me and they are not inspired by me. I am going to have to find a way to teach them anyway. My teaching fuel cannot be their approval—I have to find another fuel.

The third peak: If my trying to lead doesn't work, maybe I am going to have to learn to nip and nudge and get them focused in another way. And I'm going to have to learn to do it with conviction to calm the chaos.

The fourth peak: I have been afraid of ruining my rapport with my kids by becoming a strict, rigid disciplinarian. But I have to acknowledge that I have no rapport with my kids. There's nothing to ruin.

The fifth peak: I have to crack down firmly without it being from a place of anger, disappointment, hostility, or a desire for revenge. I am bitterly disappointed with the class, and I have days where I am resentful that my sincere efforts have netted me mainly sullen noncompliance and rowdy acting out. But I need to approach discipline from a place of calm acceptance, not reactivity. And if I have angry or cynical thoughts, at the very least I cannot let myself blame my feelings on the kids.


## The Big Crackdown

The day I choose for The Big Crackdown dawns. My principal comes in just prior to the bell, gives me a big grin and a thumbs up, and says, "Go for it! You can do it, Kat!" I read the kids the riot act. I say that, starting Wednesday, no more loaner pencils—from then on, not having a pencil will earn an infraction. I move seats around, I banish kids to the hallway, and I hand out five 3-point infractions in about 20 minutes. The kids are astonished and a bit bemused. For two days they test me relentlessly. The third day most of them settle down. Within a week the feeling in the classroom is transformed. With a few wobbles, I have managed to be matter-of-fact. I have given myself permission to take the time to do it right, to make establishing control *the* central task of the week.

It turns out that the biggest hurdle is convincing myself that I need to do it, and daring to act on the hope that this sort of discipline can come from a place of integrity and respect for my kids. I am pleasantly surprised to find that it does not seem to be experienced as an assault on their selfhood or their dignity. All but the most immature students respond well, and the most immature students end up looking just that—immature. Now it is them eliciting eye rolling from the other students, not me.

The big lesson from all this: I had to be willing to lose their approval before I could earn it. If I come into the classroom hungry for their approval, they will revolt. If I come into the classroom needing them to fill my cup, they will smash it. If my motivation to teach them is to be their savior and get their adoration, I will create a class whose primary goal becomes shattering my self-flattering dream.

Now that I'm not needing or asking for their approval, I'm starting to get it. Kids are asking to switch out of their study hall to be in my room instead. They are "tagging" my whiteboards with elaborate signatures, messages, and art. They are hanging around during free time and sometimes after school. For me, this is huge. Did I just vaporize the approval thing that has driven me my whole life?

## Lessons Beyond the Classroom

Over the next couple of months I start trying to create opportunities outside of the classroom for the students to engage with the world and hopefully ignite a spark. Two of the kids lead a diversity workshop at a teen leadership conference. Their workshop, entitled Why Are All the White Kids Sitting Together in the Cafeteria?, is the only one led by teens and is well received. The high point is when two students come to class the day after the conference and demand to know how *they* can lead a workshop like that!

I see that the years of inadequate linguistic support, frequent academic failure, and ubiquitous racism ("stupid Mexican" is a frequent epithet) have made buying into the academic enterprise way too costly for most of them. To try to join a club that rejects them and to buy into a form of success that eludes them is to risk failure and humiliation on a daily basis. To many students, rejecting school feels like the only way to salvage their dignity.

I try to help individual students move beyond this attitude but see that they keep getting sucked back into the group rejection of school, or get knocked down again by a teacher unwilling to trust in a fresh start. Trying to grab them one by one and pull them out of the peer current is an ineffective downstream intervention. We need to go upstream. That means educating the district about its failures and about the ways racism plays out in these kids' lives and affects their academic outcomes. Three of the kids do a panel presentation for teachers on being ELL students in the district. Many teachers are shocked by what they hear, and some are tendered. It is a start.

I see that we also need to create an alternative peer current for these students: a place where academic commitment will not involve leaving behind their friends or their culture. A small group agrees to form a club of aspiring college attenders. They shyly name the group *El Sueño*, "The Dream." They don't advertise meetings—some of them have been called

"White" for having academic aspirations. It is a place, I hope, where they can make it safe for each other to care about doing well.

I find in our meetings that most of them have little belief in the value of actually learning things. They see school as a series of hoops to jump through, and they have often been encouraged in this belief by teachers who have neither the time nor the inclination to help them do anything besides "get by."

I wonder if working with young kids could give my students a new perspective. I arrange for four of my students to tutor Hispanic first graders each Monday during a study hall. At first they have no idea what to do, but by the third time we go, Ramon is starting to be concerned about Jose, the little boy he is working with on spelling and vocabulary. "Boy, he's really slow," he says worriedly. "He needs a lot of help with these!" He hands me a fistful of vocabulary pictures for words Jose has not yet mastered. I am secretly elated: Ramon as Teacher is worried about Jose's comprehension. Will he start to worry about his own?

Enrique and Adriana conclude they cannot work with their own little sisters, because the girls get too silly and giggly working with their older siblings. It will be more productive, they decide, to work with other children. Will they start to notice how unproductive they are when they are with a group of friends in a study hall? Is there a way to translate Adriana's new concerns about her sister's work habits into a concern for her own?

I continue to take my students to do bilingual read-alouds to elementary students every few weeks. Maricela writes an article for the class newsletter about the experience. "I wish somebody had read to me when I was little, especially in Spanish." Will any parents reading the newsletter consider trying to read to their children? Will the kids start reading to younger siblings at home, as I have encouraged them to do? Can I get more students to see it as a personal pleasure and a part of their family culture rather than a school thing?

## Becoming Agents of Change

The local newspaper does a poll of readers, asking how common racism is in Ripon. The readership, almost exclusively White, weighs in confidently. I share the results with my students, who laugh derisively at the poll's underestimate of the extent of racism. I invite them to respond with letters to the editor. The letters are printed, and the principal gets a phone call from a community member asking what the school is doing about the racism that the students experience. The students are proud and elated to see their views published. Will this experience help motivate them to invest further in their communicative effectiveness?

I sign up a couple of van loads of kids—Anglo, Hispanic, and Black—for the upcoming White Privilege Conference. My hope is that it will take my students to the next step, becoming agents of change. I hope they will meet activists who will show them another version of the American Dream: achieving meaning and success through empowerment and social commitment rather than merely acquisition of material goods.

I can't say we've reached the Promised Land together, but we have a solid working relationship. Some of the kids are reading for pleasure and telling me about the books. Some of them have signed up for tutors and residential summer schools. Some members of El Sueño recently took the ACT for the first time and had their first college tour. And these days, almost all of my students can be counted on to bring a pencil to class.

## Journal Questions

1. Kat says in her piece, "I had moments of introspection over the fact that I was lavishing all my energy and first-rate education on very few kids—kids who were going to do fine with or without me. I did not feel I was furthering social justice or living the dream I'd had." In your journal write your best argument for or against teaching as social justice work.

2. Kat says she wrestled with an addiction to approval. In your journal, based on Kat's writings and your own personal life, write the diagnostic criteria for an "approval addict."

3. Write this headline in your journal: "White Teachers Scared to Let Students of Color Get Together for Fear They Might Lose Control." Underneath, write an article to go with the headline.

4. Describe in your journal what fuels your teaching.

5. You have just heard a panel of English language learner (ELL) students present on what it is like to be an ELL student in your district. In your journal write your reaction to what the students said.

# 5

# MY ALL-AMERICAN
# BIRTHRIGHT

*Rachel Stephens*

"Mrs. Johnson looked at me with cold eyes and started listing all the reasons why the Academy of Westland needed to have more Black teachers teaching at the school. She was direct and said, 'You don't understand Black children or their families.' She then accused me of being too young and White to teach African American children."

I've come to realize that one reason new teachers are naïve about teaching in an urban area is because they grow up in a whitewashed community with no contact with anyone different from themselves. Whiteness everywhere—despite having technology that puts us in contact with anyone, anywhere on the planet, we have no physical reality that challenges our White worldview. From the time we are a baby we are tacitly instructed that we are the norm and everyone who is not like us is different and therefore somehow suspect. Growing up in Owosso/Corunna, Michigan, with a population of 23,000 people, I didn't consciously think these things or decide to believe in their truth—this was my White birthright.

As a child I could walk along the Shiawassee River, pass the Curwood Castle, and dream of being the princess who lives there. Owosso is one of those idyllic Midwest towns that protects us from all that isn't like us through cultural uniformity. I accepted my community's idea of how people live: in an intact family with two parents, a home, and a sibling or two. My 1998 Corunna High School's graduating class had 160 students, almost all

White. Like many of the White friends I grew up with, we carry around a subtle racism, a gift from our segregated upbringing.

My identity as a woman who represents any American woman seemed as natural as being someone's daughter; I had the privilege of not having to think about my identity as being White. My mother stayed at home, was involved in our school life, and protected me from any threat of hardship. She made sure I did not experience academic failure, letting me know I could be whatever I wanted to be and would be successful at it. I could not see that I was raced and had a culture from which I derived advantage by practicing White cultural norms.

I experienced myself as being unraced, both special and average, lacking ethnicity—and a critical conscience. That identity of self followed me to Grand Valley State University (GVSU), where I finally came into contact with people not like me. For the first time in my life I ventured into a world of diversity and opened up to a racial consciousness.

## Awareness of Cultural Difference

When I arrived at GVSU my life consisted of one narrative: the perky, enthusiastic, eager, and earnest young woman ready to go forth into the world and make a difference. I wanted adventure and yearned to move out of the commonness I felt but couldn't explain. I ended up involved in various programs, including Hope Network in Grand Rapids, Big Brothers Big Sisters, and Gleaners Food Bank. Any program that required working with low-income adults and children became fascinating to me. I spent many hours working in shelters or day cares that catered to homeless or low-income mothers and children. Other programs such as Big Brothers Big Sisters allowed me to impact and make a difference in an individual child's life. I enjoyed packing boxes at Gleaners knowing that a needy family would benefit from the items received, and I felt that I had power to make a difference. I had a tiny understanding that race and poverty was systematized to keep people separated and that, if I could give up being scared, I could join a much bigger circle of humanity. Somehow I knew that would make my life more meaningful.

I didn't realize it then, but making my life more meaningful starts on the inside. What I saw in these programs was children with needs, and I wanted to be the person who could satisfy those needs. I wanted to swoop in and show these children that they never needed to be disappointed with White people because we could change the world for them. I never actually heard myself say words like "these children" and "for them"; I just wanted to help. This is when my resolve to work with low-income students began.

## Academy of Westland, Westland, Michigan (2003–2006)

My reaction to my first teaching contract was, "Wow, now I can finally teach and make a living at it." I no longer *wanted to be* a teacher, I *was* a teacher, and I resolved to make a difference by working with low-income children.

I had graduated from Eastern Michigan University in December of 2003 and sent my resume to the Academy of Westland in Westland, Michigan, that same month. I should have been surprised when I received a call from the principal the same day they received my resume, but I wasn't. I was confident someone would hire me. It was expected of me by my professors, my family, and everyone who knew me—I would get a job.

As I walked into the Academy of Westland for my interview, I was excited to meet with the principal. I had never faced any big failures; people had never shunned me for anything I did. I had been accepted for being me, and my confidence outweighed my fear. After interviewing with the principal I was offered the kindergarten teacher position in a class of predominantly Black students. It was a full-day program, and the majority of students came from the neighborhood of Inkster. Some were bused in from the city of Detroit, mostly low-income children and African Americans. I thought, *This is where I want to be.*

The school was an old building with cream-colored bricks and a small network of cracks etched on the walls like overworked veins. From the front entrance, a long hallway stretched out for what seemed like miles. Glass showcases were situated throughout the building, and some of the floor-to-ceiling windows with brick sills had been replaced by a pair of smaller, newer windows. Still, the grandeur of the place remained, and although it was not necessarily a clean building, the staff had put a great amount of effort into decorating the school walls to create an energetic learning environment.

As I toured the building with the principal, the feeling of being filled with gratitude made me a little wobbly, but I knew I was grounded in my desire to blaze the right trail. I heard myself say, "Wow, this is great! I have actually made it. I will be in a school where I can give kids a chance." I was a real teacher, teaching children who needed *me*. As I stood in the hall, joy saturated my skin and I smiled a smile that spread over half my face.

I started in January of 2004, right after Christmas. Family and friends, anticipating that there are no everyday school supplies in urban schools, gave me several teacher store certificates for Christmas; with them I purchased basic classroom supplies. Before I arrived, my class of kindergartners had gone through four teachers, so I knew they would be distrustful of me at first. But I also knew I would be the last teacher they saw this year; it would be a matter of convincing them they could count on me.

I still remember walking into my very own classroom that Monday morning. I carried my professional-looking book bag draped over my shoulder, and I was all dressed up and ready to teach 5-year-olds. The cavernous size of my classroom with two floor-to-ceiling windows opened up a world of opportunities for me and my charges. The room was bare, with no sign that any students had inhabited the space, so I set about to change my classroom into a bright and cheery environment.

Over the course of that month I arranged and rearranged displays, hung decorations, and spent hours prepping and planning. Of course, I wanted to create a classroom that was "multicultural," so I put up posters of Martin Luther King Jr. and a Black History Month calendar and placed a smattering of books with children of color as main characters throughout the room.

Throughout the year I created hands-on lessons with diversity as a recurring theme and made sure the students knew I held African Americans in high esteem. As I look back I realize I felt totally competent in creating diverse experiences for my students. After all, I was a multicultural teacher.

## Parent/Teacher Conferences: Not Everyone Wants a White Teacher (November 2004)

I had just begun my second year of teaching at the Academy of Westland. I was still considered a new teacher after having taught only a half-year, but my confidence in my teaching ability anchored me in hopes for a great second year. I was sure I had a great classroom of kindergartners, and that the 2004/2005 school year was going to be productive.

The physical space in my classroom was emblematic of some innovative ideas I had come up with during the summer. I anxiously awaited fall parent-teacher conferences to share with parents what I was doing for their child. The previous year I had had little contact with most of the students' parents, having missed conferences and knowing single parents don't have time for meetings after school. But this year I was sure to see my students' parents at conferences.

After four conferences that I believed went well because the parents expressed gratitude that their child was progressing, I met with the mother of a shy but well-behaved student, Monique Johnson. Mrs. Johnson walked into the classroom and sat down at the table. I began, "Monique struggles with grasping certain concepts." In my mind, this child must have been lacking an "enriched environment" at home. But because I didn't want the conversation to be negative, I added, "But Monique is one of my best worker bees and is great at following directions."

The mother did not say anything and I was unable to gauge her thoughts or feelings on her daughter's progress, so I continued, "I need to tell you that your daughter struggles when learning her alphabet letters and sounds, shapes, and numbers." I now could sense an attitude surfacing in the mother and I was completely unaware of why she might have an attitude. I was helping her understand where her child was academically. I thought I could derail comments about my teaching and began to explain the importance of working with Monique at home.

Mrs. Johnson looked at me with cold eyes and started listing all the reasons why the Academy of Westland needed to have more Black teachers teaching at the school. She was direct and said, "You don't understand Black children or their families." She then accused me of being too young and White to teach African American children.

I was on the verge of tears but refused to cry in front of her; I was better than that. This particular incident was not something they had prepared me for in college. Nor was this something I thought would occur to someone determined to teach low-income, minority children. I let the mother finish talking and then politely said that I was sorry she felt this way. I was shaking and my stomach was in knots. Mrs. Johnson left after I gave her the child's report card. I wanted to be done with conferences at that moment but had parents waiting in the hall.

I knew I never wanted to have another parent-teacher conference like the one that just occurred. By the end of the night I felt emotionally drained from conferences. I was thankful that the rest of my meetings went smoothly. Driving home that night I continued to reflect on Mrs. Johnson and why she seemed to hate me. I spent the whole night thinking about it. I was really bothered and offended by her accusations. All I wanted was for her daughter to be successful in my classroom. Why put her anger on me?

The following week Mrs. Johnson's words kept coming back at me: "You can't teach Black children." I thought that maybe if I knew more about Mrs. Johnson I might understand her, so I set out to find information about this Johnson family. I discovered that Monique's mother was a single parent and that her father was uninvolved. She was the eldest child of three. Her mother was raising her and two other small children, working two jobs, and living in a less-than-ideal apartment. She was truly trying her best as a parent, and I should have acknowledged this during conferences. I did not have a full understanding of the struggles my student's family was facing and the possible reasons for her low academic performance in my classroom.

The truth appeared to be that Mrs. Johnson was so busy trying to keep food on the table and to raise three small children that she needed me on *her* side more than I needed her on mine. Her accusations were correct. I truly had no idea where she was coming from or why her child was struggling academically. No wonder she had decided I couldn't teach Black children.

This incident taught me a lot about my classroom practices. First, I became aware that I needed to know more about my students and their families. I had to have some understanding of my students' backgrounds to help them become successful in my classroom. Second, I quickly learned to present a child's struggles in my classroom in a different light to his or her parent(s). Even if they are responsible for their child's academic or behavioral struggles, I needed allies, not enemies. I did recognize that I will never have full understanding because my skin is white and I did not have the same struggles my students were having growing up. This parent-teacher conference incident even helped to change the environment of my classroom. I created extra opportunities for my struggling students, knowing that many parents were unable to work with their child at home. I would allow extra time for students to work in small groups, work with my paraprofessional in the classroom, and even tutor students after school. I truly loved each of my students and wanted them to be successful.

## Discipline Differs Between Cultures (February 2006)

My third year of teaching I had a student, JuWon, who had a classroom behavior problem. At random times during the course of the school year his mother, Ms. Robinson, would stop by during the day. She would check on his progress and behavior. Although Ms. Robinson was usually supportive, I was left with the nagging feeling that she thought I didn't know when and how to discipline her child because I was White. One day while I was lining up my students for lunch Ms. Robinson came into my classroom. All the students had promptly positioned themselves in line except JuWon. He wasn't paying attention to me or the task at hand, so he wasn't in line. Ms. Robinson walked in, saw him clowning around, walked over to JuWon, pulled a belt out of her purse, and gave him a whooping right there in the classroom in front of the other students.

Nineteen 5-year-olds and one 27-year-old woman stood silent, frozen in line, staring at this mother belting her child. As I stood there holding my breath, I knew the problem was with me. I hadn't realized how differently African American parents from other cultures discipline their children and should have been ready for this potential scenario. In all my years of elementary, middle, and high school I have never seen a parent come into the classroom and whoop their child. During my student teaching in the Detroit public schools I had heard stories of parents whooping kids, but I never encountered a situation like this. I finally realized that I and the other students hadn't moved an inch. Finally, I looked at the students in line and firmly said, "Let's move on to lunch, children," leaving Ms. Robinson and JuWon alone in the classroom.

At some level I felt I should have said something to Ms. Robinson, like "Can you do this in another room?" or "I don't allow hitting in my classroom," but I was uncomfortable saying anything to her because I was young, White, and bright enough to know I was too ignorant about child-rearing practices in the African American family to say anything. Once my students were settled in the lunch room, I walked back to my classroom and was relieved to see that Ms. Robinson and JuWon had left my classroom. I went straight to my desk, sat down, and put my hands over my face. I felt like a foreigner in a strange land.

First, I was disappointed in myself. I was not able to manage my classroom because of this one particular student's behavior. Was I really being an effective teacher to all my African American students? Why couldn't I even manage just one student's behavior? Second, I realized that I did not know as much about the African American culture from my two years of teaching as I had thought. If I was naïve about discipline styles, what else had I assumed or presumed about the culture?

It was at this moment that I realized I needed to know more about how cultures discipline children at home and how this can have an impact in my classroom. Maybe I needed to become more firm when disciplining my students and manage my entire classroom better, with clear rules and consequences that all students understood. I decided my young kindergartners needed to spend time reviewing classroom expectations and consequences over the course of the school year. This particular incident opened my eyes to the differences in discipline styles between two cultures and to my own classroom management system.

## South Arbor Charter Academy: Opportunity for Growth

I left the Academy of Westland after three years when I was offered a contract at South Arbor Charter Academy in Ypsilanti, Michigan. This was a great opportunity with the National Heritage Charter Academies. South Arbor operated with the philosophy that students need a structured academic environment that provides a rigorous curriculum. The school believed a child's moral development is as important as his or her academics, and we worked to support our parents' efforts to instill character in their children. The school did this by reinforcing and demonstrating universal virtues such as integrity, wisdom, courage, and respect.

At South Arbor I taught the first graders who were grouped as the lowest performing students. My class was predominantly White students, and was a very different environment than at Westland. The parents were supportive and expected to be actively involved with the school. Although I loved my South Arbor students, I wasn't working with low-income children, which was my true passion.

However, teaching at South Arbor Academy afforded me an opportunity I never imagined having as that White girl from Owosso. Any teacher in the school interested in doing a teacher exchange program could travel to another country to teach. I was chosen to teach in Tanzania, Africa, and spent three weeks during the summer of 2009 learning teacher strategies for and insight into Tanzania's culture. On June 26, 2009, another teacher, two women I did not know well, and I boarded an airplane for Dar es Salaam, Tanzania. As we departed the Detroit Metro Airport my entire body was overwhelmed with feelings of insecurity, excitement, fear, and joy, knowing that in 18 hours I would be in a third-world country. It was an opportunity to reach a milestone in my teaching career, but that did not prevent me from feeling anxious and afraid. What would happen, how would I be accepted, and would I come back a truly different multicultural teacher?

Two days later I found myself on top of a van rumbling over a dry, bumpy, dusty road through astonishing and unfamiliar terrain. We ended up at Kibangu English Middle School. Kibangu was a private pre-primer (preschool) to grade seven where the students had to speak their second language at school: English. Our first week in Dar es Salaam, the students were on their holiday break. My coteacher and I had the job of organizing and assigning grade level to the books in the library, a task neither of us had ever done before, so it would be functioning by the time we departed for home. Kibangu had a building that was dedicated to the library, which was extremely rare for any school in Africa, and the school had received a great number of donated books from the Books for Africa organization.

We spent many hours unpacking boxes of books and deciding what grade level they were appropriate for, keeping in mind that English was all the students' second language. On the second day of sorting and leveling I was casually flipping through the books and realized that some of them were worthless to the children at Kibangu: A number of them had to be tossed because they were in Spanish. Others were stories about American or European students whose experiences were thousands of miles, both literally and metaphorically, from the students we would be teaching. The students would find it almost impossible to make any kind of connection with the experiences in these books.

I came across all kinds of donated books that were not appropriate for the wonderful children of Kibangu, and I was becoming angry and upset with the people who had sorted and donated the books: What were they thinking? How did they imagine these students could learn from these books? Suddenly, tears came to my eyes. As I sat in the dusty little library in Tanzania and became upset with people who had had good intentions when they donated these books, I also realized that, for the past six years, I had done the very same thing in my classroom.

I guess I was crying for me—a teacher who was so naïve about what composes a multicultural classroom and what constitutes multicultural teaching. But I was also crying because of the humiliation I was experiencing in that moment. I had felt good about what I did in my "multicultural classroom" because of my good intentions, but now I was seeing that I hadn't truly understood or accurately perceived the needs of my students. Like the book donors, I did not embrace the truth of my students' lives or understand their culture.

As I tossed one book after another into a bin for destinations unknown, I realized that I should have tossed some of the shallow approaches I had taken to presenting multicultural learning in my classroom. How I wished now that I had grappled with really understanding the children in my classroom. It was just easier on my fragile teacher self to live with the confidence and belief that I knew what I was doing. It was easier than confronting my ignorance to believe multicultural teaching is putting up Black History bulletin boards, having your students color in pictures of Dr. Martin Luther King Jr., or putting a few children's storybooks with African American characters in them in your library.

The following two weeks in Africa were very busy as I worked in many teachers' classrooms modeling lessons. Although my days were filled with questions from teachers, hugs from students, and planning lessons for the children at Kibangu, I was unable to stop thinking about my own teaching practices back home.

I knew I had to change my teaching practices to accommodate the needs of all of my students and to create a learning environment where each student would be successful. I was filled with excitement thinking about the new school year approaching, yet sad that I hadn't implemented successful multicultural practices with the students I had taught the past five years.

## Heading Home (July 28, 2009)

When my coworker and I boarded the plane for Michigan we were leaving a piece of our hearts in Tanzania with the wonderful people there who had embraced us. What I wanted now was simply a piece of pizza, some Mexican food, and a chance to be with my family. Although my desire for certain foods had not changed, I knew I was coming home a changed teacher. The poverty-stricken country of Tanzania had forever changed my ideas of what it meant to be a "good teacher," and I knew I would forever be grateful to its people and its land.

When I walked into my classroom for the 2009/2010 school year I knew that I would see my students, my colleagues, and the physical classroom from a very different vantage point. I was ready to start the new school year and create a truly multicultural classroom that would challenge my students to learn and would begin the challenge from the starting point of each student.

Back at South Arbor Charter Academy, I continued longing to teach in a lower income school. That passion for working with poor kids had now been with me for more than 10 years, and I wanted to answer my life's calling. In August of 2010 I got the call to be a first-grade teacher at Metro Academy in Romulus, Michigan. Metro Academy's demographics were unlike South Arbor's, with about 65 percent of the students receiving free and reduced-price lunches. My renewed journey of working in multicultural schools began at Metro, where 26 of my students were African American and three were White.

I was thrilled to be a teacher at Metro, but being there made me long for a "do over" of my first three years at the Academy of Westland. I had been naïve and filled with expectations and assumptions that were actually misconceptions. But I also believe I garnered many insights from having those years to reflect back on. How would I have known the difference, given my early cultural experiences?

My new perspective on creating a multicultural classroom is not a paint-by-the-numbers approach. I reach all my students by creating differentiated units, and I carefully examine the curriculum used in the classroom to revise instruction materials if something isn't working. I also have no *amour propre* invested in analyzing and reflecting on my own bias and stereotypes in the classroom. I need to check and recheck where my thinking is coming from.

I also now know the power of collaborating and working with colleagues and local community members. For my classroom environment to be successful it has to be a place where students embrace their individual differences and similarities and those of other students. The classroom then serves as a geographic location where every student enjoys learning from a multicultural perspective.

## Journal Questions

1. Rachel says college did not prepare her for the hostility she encountered as a White teacher. Have you had such an encounter? How did you react? Write in your journal about it or an encounter you witnessed another White teacher experiencing.

2. How, specifically, do we make a "multicultural classroom" if what Rachel tried is not enough? Journal about what you would like to know about making a classroom genuinely multicultural.

*Nancy Peterson with husband Chester
at her retirement party from Minneapolis
Public Schools, June 2008*

6

# THE SCREEN DOOR

### Race Around an Ordinary Life

*Nancy Peterson*

"When I started teaching, I knew that I could work with the children; this was my role in this bigger picture of social justice. I worked hard and kept a low profile. After one year there, one of the African American mothers made a comment to others that she liked me. She seemed surprised that she felt this way."

### THE SCREEN DOOR

*Race around an ordinary life
Is a screen door people look through but seldom open
I am a white woman behind the screen door
trying to talk
I am a white woman trying to talk
about race
Scared
I am a scared white woman trying
Introvert
I am a scared white woman introvert
Interracially married
I am an interracially married scared white woman
introvert trying to talk about race*

*Ain't I a strong woman?
Dare I open that screen door?*

## I Am a Scared White Woman Trying to Talk About Race . . .

My cultural sensitivity grew in my life through experiences of pain and joy. These awakened me to a richer world shared with people of color. My life story went from a secure but isolated Polish Catholic childhood to an interracial marriage and raising two daughters who consider themselves citizens of the world. After growing up in Minneapolis, my daughters attended Howard University in Washington, DC, which had a lot to do with that new gestalt.

Working with young children comes as second nature to me maybe because I did so much babysitting when I was young. I have always been more comfortable with children than with adults. I gravitate toward them at gatherings. They are usually freer to interact and give their gifts. As I sit with them, and listen and reflect back their actions and discoveries, they do more and give more. I learned at midlife that an adult's "reflecting back" is what gives children a sense of self, being seen as they are and having that reflected back to them by the adults in their lives.

When I student-taught middle-school-age kids, I didn't understand their impudence. When I was young, we were not allowed to be. We obeyed and were silent in school, giggling in the choir loft our only trespass.

Truthfulness, kindness to those not befriended by others, and innocence were the virtues I knew. They were not taught directly, but we lived them in the insular upbringing of Polish Catholics. I still carry these and am taken aback when people display the opposite. I didn't and don't understand deceit, mockery, or doing good only for yourself and not for others.

When I went to the University of Minnesota for six years during the late '60s, my world expanded and my eyes were opened to the changes of the times. But I still clung to a naïveté about how "all of us getting along" should be easy. In reality, my limited relationship to people of color included paternalism and pity paired with a strong belief in justice for all.

In 1977 at age 30, I married Chester, an African American man, and at the same time began my career as an early childhood special education teacher with the Minneapolis Public Schools. My marriage and this work were the beginning of a life of change for me.

My teaching has been mainly with children of color with special needs. As a special education teacher, it was so easy to tell parents what was wrong with their child and what they might do to help. But if I were seen as the expert, what would parents have to contribute, and how would my knowledge fit into the reality of their daily routine with their child and the rest of their experience?

I was faced with racism when I stepped out with my family, if not overtly at least with the looks we got, the head turning we caused. Chester said, "Of course we turn heads. They are noticing how beautiful we are." This is typical of him. He is a person of great self-confidence, who can be himself and traverse in two cultures, the Black and the White. He came from inner-city St. Louis to Minnesota to attend St. John's University in Collegeville. It doesn't matter to him what others say or think about us. But I felt very vulnerable. I faded myself to the background in my African American family. Why did I not talk about my Polish and Swedish heritage and make it as prominent as the African American side of our family?

I've always had a strong longing to belong. I wanted people to like me, but also deep down I wanted to make a difference in the world. I participated in the Milwaukee march for fair housing with Father Groppi, and was so excited to be part of this movement that involved my feet and my heart. An interracial group, we were all singing and marching together. I became part of something that made a difference and was bigger than myself. I heard Rev. Jesse Jackson talk passionately about the Rainbow Coalition. There were many strong visual images of this interracial coalition on TV in the voting rights and civil rights marches in the south. We could join hands with Dr. King and Jesse Jackson. White people also had their martyrs for the cause during this time. The Catholic premise of my childhood, that we were all created equal, was starting to come true. I had a sense of social justice and wanted to be part of doing good in the world. I became a part and apart—straddling the fence and seeing both sides. This is a great vantage point, and I could climb down either side of the fence and join either group.

But when in 1968 I attended sessions for White people given by Black Power advocates, I felt apart and deeply shamed. I was no longer able to contribute to the movement. I was part of the White establishment, and my part in social justice was rejected. As a White liberal, feeling shame and guilt, I felt powerless and knew I had no place in the movement. I was stuck in that place for many years.

## I Am a Scared White Woman . . .

When I met Chester I could see his goodness and his ability to live in two worlds and still be true to himself; I saw this as possible for myself. When I got to know him better and saw that he called his mama every week and tried to help his brothers get out of St. Louis and the drug scene, I knew more of his goodness. When he fixed me whiting fish and sweet potato pie in his kitchen, I knew he could be a partner. When he didn't flinch when others reacted to our relationship in a negative way, I knew it was possible.

Once I had jumped the first hurdle by dating Chester, I was in for the whole run. The other hurdles—my parents not coming to our wedding, the whispers by good White liberals of "What about the children?", the discomfort in public, knowing people were stereotyping us—I would jump too. I knew we had a good thing, something real, meaningful, and bigger than the both of us.

> *Are we kin, my Cheslov?*
> *Am I your little Anansi?*
> *We search for threads,*
> *Connections of a common history,*
> *On the banks of the muddy Mississippi,*
> *Singin' the blues.*

(Cheslov is Chester in Polish, and the African spider-storyteller Anansi is often called Nancy.)

## I Am a White Woman Behind the Screen Door

Father Janicke was the new parish priest at St. Philip's, my Polish Catholic church in north Minneapolis, when I was in high school. When he started with our Legion of Mary group, we prayed the rosary at each meeting and made holy water bottles and baptismal gowns. He gradually turned our eyes from downcast to straight out into the world. I went from my knees to my feet, marching for fair housing. I was so elated to be part of this movement and to feel we could make a difference.

In my sophomore year in college, I lived in a community of women at Wesley Center on the University of Minnesota campus. My roommate was a Black woman and we were friendly with each other but not close. One evening, I was lying in bed and she came into our room with her boyfriend. She very mockingly said, "I know you are really awake." She was right but I didn't open my eyes. I felt trapped in my own shame. They laughed and made out for a while before they left again. I froze in place and felt humiliated. Why did I not say something then—or ever—about the incident? I thought, in my own distorted way, that because she was Black, I didn't have the right to be angry at her or to ever say anything about it. I know that influenced our relationship from then on. I didn't think about how she might feel an outsider, living in this community as the only African American woman. Was this her way of expressing her alienation, as my way was going into my shame?

## Are We Kin, My Cheslov?

Chester and I met at work in 1975 at Parent Child Center, a federal program for birth-to-3-year-old children and their families. He had just gotten his master's in social work from the University of Minnesota. He had come from inner-city St. Louis six years earlier to attend St. John's University.

What a culture shock it must have been for him riding the Greyhound from St. Louis to Collegeville, Minnesota. Chester survived St. John's by hanging out with foreign students and the few other African Americans, who came from St. Louis, Chicago, and the Caribbean. And when enrolled in the MSW program at the University of Minnesota, he had some Jewish women faculty looking out for him. They supported him in his choice to continue, and helped him find work, including a job with Gisela Konopka's Center for Youth Development and Research at the University of Minnesota (aka the Parent Child Center).

When he walked into Parent Child Center, he was wearing his backpack and looking like a young student, and I was sitting in the office drawing a Big Bird poster and smoking a Kent. He became part of the administrative team, which was all African American, and I was one of the White teachers in the trenches. I had thought it unfair that the administrators got to go to all the retreats and workshops paid for with federal money and the teachers didn't, so when he asked me if I wanted to go to the center's dinner at the hotel, I said yes. Before this, we had related as siblings, bantering and teasing each other. That night, after dinner and dancing, I stayed the night with him in the hotel and snuck out in the morning.

The week after the dinner at the hotel, I told Chester, "We need to talk about our relationship. Don't be chicken." Then he took up my challenge. We were on scary ground. We were in love and were going to make it work.

We kept our relationship secret at work, but one morning when they called Chester's apartment, his brother told them he was "at Nancy's"! The word was out. No one talked directly to either of us about it, but we knew there were whisperings. Black and White dating was not okay. In the population of poor families we served, the White women who had biracial children were often struggling, and their children were considered by staff to be "a little mixed up."

Also, relations between Black and White people in this setting were not social. When I started teaching, I knew that I could work with the children; this was my role in this bigger picture of social justice. I worked hard and kept a low profile. After one year there, one of the African American mothers made a comment to others that she liked me. She seemed surprised that she felt this way. It exemplified the separation, the gulf between the races, that it took her a whole year of associating with me to begin to like me a little.

## We Come From Different Roots

Chester and I were married on August 20, 1977.

After we announced to our friends our plans to be married, some of Chester's Black women friends expressed their disapproval of his marrying a White woman. Chester understood why they were feeling that way. They began to call him less, and we saw them only occasionally after we were married. When we did I always felt cautious. I knew many Black women felt anger about Black men being with White women.

> *Friendship with a black woman*
> *Crossing the color line*
> *I keep my distance*
> *Out of range of some eyes*
> *I take on the white man's demeanor*
> *And devil fear walks along side*
> *I want a new companion*
> *Walk me over the line*
> *Cool drink of water*
> *Waits on the other side*
>
> *I kept my distance*
> *Out of range of some eyes*
> *I took on that white man's demeanor*
> *Condescend (to stoop)*
> *Patronize (father)*
> *Guilt (remorse for a crime)*
> *Pity (pieta)*
> *Anxiety (narrowness)*
> *These kept me from stepping forward*
> *Over that line.*

*I want a new language*
*I'm through with those lines*
*I want a new companion*
*Walk me over the line*
*Cool drink of water*
*Waits on the other side*

## *Polish Roots*

We tried to hide our relationship from my parents. I knew my mother would be incensed. One Saturday morning as Chester was going down the steps of my apartment, guitar in hand, my parents were coming up the stairs. They thought they'd surprise me.

"Mom and Dad, this is my friend Chester."

"How do you do. Oh, you play the guitar?"

Chester greeted them and then he walked out the door. My parents and I didn't even mention him during the rest of their visit. Later that year, when I told them we would be married, I knew I was cutting myself off from them. Mom would not accept my marrying a Black man. I felt deeply hurt by this and it was a wrenching moment when I told them. My mother said, "We can't come. We just can't come."

## *African American Roots*

Early in our relationship I had taken the train to St. Louis to meet Chester's family. His mother, Bernice, had only wanted to know if I was taller than him! When I leaned down to hug her, she knew. She is five-foot-one and I am five-nine. Chester's brothers embraced me in their kitchen. I felt at home in her home. When Bernice and I went to the Veteran's Thrift Store in her neighborhood it was a different story. As we were walking through the aisles of the thrift store, I was hit in the head with a basketball from out of nowhere. We didn't see the person throwing it, but I got the message that I was not welcome. I cried about it later in Bernice's kitchen.

We had Chester's family and my sisters, we became part of an interracial community that was vibrant and healthy, and we found a Quaker community that accepted and loved us. We grew as a family, with lovely talented daughters, and we created a "play family"—friends and elders that became like family. It is common in African American families to create "play" family members. We had "adopted" John Lutz, an African American elder who was a painter and wood carver, as a grandfather to our girls. They didn't have a "real" African American grandfather in their lives, and he was willing to step in.

On a visit to my parents' home before we were married, I bought the old sewing machine and piano from them because I knew I wouldn't inherit them. I went to the garage and looked at the antique knife-sharpening wheel and knew my children would not see this, and maybe not know their sweet Grampa who spun it. I took a walk down the dirt road with Dad before I left. He told me he could tell that Chester and I loved each other. He told me he loved me, but he couldn't come to the wedding because mother would not come. So I didn't invite my extended family to our wedding, only my three sisters and their families. All of Chester's family pulled up in their cars from St. Louis that week in August 1977 to celebrate with us. From the beginning, they have always fully embraced me.

In our wedding vows we said:

> *We come from different roots.*
> *As man and woman, as black and white.*
> *We share an affinity for music, dreams, children, grits and yogurt.*
> *We go towards a life growing in trust and respect.*
> *Trust in being close and vulnerable.*
> *Respect in each other's uniqueness.*
> *We move towards making ourselves more whole.*
> *We look forward towards a family.*
> *At this moment we want to acknowledge our love*
> *and support for one another,*
> *And share our hopes and fears with you close to us.*
> *And thank you for supporting us in our life together.*

We have carried out those promises, with the grace of God, for the 32 years we have been married.

In early spring of 1978 I visited my parents with my three sisters, but Chester did not come. Someone mentioned that I was pregnant, and mom commented sarcastically to me, "Oh, I hear you're going to have a family." On the way home in the car, I started to bleed. I had a miscarriage that night when I got home. Did I blame my mother for the miscarriage? Though unspoken, I probably did.

A get-together was scheduled for Mother's Day that same spring, and my sisters planned a boycott. They told my mother, "If we come to celebrate with you, the whole family comes. If we come, Chester comes." She reluctantly said yes, and Chester was with us for Mother's Day. This was the beginning of my parents and I reestablishing our relationship.

Our first daughter, Meghan, was born in January 1979, and she broke down the barriers that had blocked the love between my parents and me. My parents came that summer to hold her and to see her walk down the sidewalk in front of our home in the diverse neighborhood of north Minneapolis.

In November 1979, awaiting the birth of our second daughter, Hannah, my parents came to help us fix the house. There was no talk of the pain from the past, but love was expressed by their hands as they helped us wash the tar and nicotine off of the walls in the living room.

Ten years later Chester and his mother, the girls, and I went to visit my parents. We brought along the wedding pictures. We all looked at the pictures and expressed regret for what they had missed and how they were missed at the celebration. Time heals some wounds.

Race was paramount on my mind that day because this was the first time Chester's mother had visited their lake home. I was happily surprised by mom's reception of her, and when I watched them at a distance sitting on the dock together, the way they leaned into their talk, I could have mistaken them for sisters. Later, at her garden:

> Mom, you pose happily by your garden,
> your raison d'être,
> with your family of many colors.
> You welcome Bernice with open arms
> and fresh blueberry pie.
> You two spend much time together,
> talking coupons and the price of bacon,
> talking children and "Is he a saint, too?"

## We Search for Threads

In the early 1990s Chester and I were two of the presenters in a citywide interracial family workshop. Dr. Anita Brooks opened the conference talking about the roles and relationships between Black men and White women, Black women and White men, that started in the time and culture of enslavement. Some of those underlying assumptions, buried hurts, relationships, and perceptions are still present today, she said. It was difficult to hear those definitive words and see the visual diagrams about these exploitive and degrading relationships and to think that some of this has not left us.

Chester and I participated in an interracial family conference, and I was to speak about being part of an interracial family. I was feeling very nervous about speaking and fearful of what the audience reaction might be. Before the conference began Dr. Brooks came up to me and said, "Don't be looking for acceptance here. You are just fine." She spoke to my condition. That's exactly what was going on for me. I was not aware that my underlying and unspoken motivation to speak included, "See, we are a healthy family. We love each other. We are aware and know what to do for our children." Her words before I spoke helped me afterward, when I felt attacked and vulnerable. When the floor was opened for questions and comments, a Black woman said to me, "Why did you take the cream of the crop? You could have married a Dayton."

THE WHITE BUTTERFLY

*Her question projected,*
*a sword swift and hot,*
*with no ear for a response,*
*no ear for my silent wail*
*but only hearing the wind off the blade,*
*finely polished*
*and sharpened daily*
*by her life as a black woman in America,*
*by her pain*
*looking for a target.*
*The tip of the blade finds my heart.*

*"Do you understand racism?"*
*"Love is irrelevant."*
*"You dilute the race."*
*You do not belong here*
*Except pinned to the wall.*

I can laugh to myself about it now. "Me? Marry a Dayton? Me, from the Polish northside working-class Catholic neighborhood, marry from the upper-class family that owns Dayton's department stores?"

Being in an interracial family, I sought some connection with the Black community and some friendships across the color line. Even *with* this connection, I find myself settling into my Quaker community and my neighborhood, which are both 99 percent Caucasian. I have to make a conscious effort to go to a different neighborhood or a different culture's grocery store or restaurant, attend an event run by a different ethnic group, or attend meetings and offer support to the Northside Peace Foundation.

## You Dilute the Race

We identified as an interracial family and as a Black family. It was important to Chester to raise Meghan Aisha and Hannah Jamila with a Black identity. This is how society would see them and treat them. They would experience racism and needed a strong Black identity. I took on being invisible in my family. But Chester's love helped me to grow and to make this scary and powerful journey. I began to tell the girls stories about my Swedish and Polish relatives and to affirm my own identity. Over many years, I gained my own voice and took risks to be out there as myself, speaking my ideas about race and feeling more grounded when they differed from Chester's ideas.

Chester and I became Quakers when the girls were in preschool, and in the Midwest there are few Friends of color. Chester is often the only Black person at meeting. In 1991 the Fellowship of Friends of African Descent met for the first time, at Pendle Hill outside of Philadelphia. Everyone who gathered there from across the United States, and one from South Africa, was so grateful to meet other Quakers of color and their families that the group has continued to meet biannually since then.

At one business meeting during the 2000 Jamaica gathering, it was decided not to mention that there were Caucasian Americans who had attended. I was hurt and, very unlike me, I said something about it. There was a heated discussion, including "Why do Caucasians always have to own/put their stamp on everything? Listen to the name of this organization: 'The Fellowship of Friends of African Descent!'" Afterward, I approached Aibi Reed, an African American Quaker from California, and asked if we could talk about this. We met over ackee fish and rice, and she said, "This is not the place to work on your invisibility issue. See this experience as all good. This is a humbling experience for you. Be here in humility. Pray about it."

She was right. I was there as a guest. This was their organization. This was a hard lesson for me because, in my personal journey, I was working on being more visible. She loved me in this message and I felt her love. I heard her and took it to my heart.

> *Now riding on the hot rail of race,*
> *we attempt to speak our truth.*
> *We know our places of muddle*
> *but say it anyway.*

At the end of the weekend, Chester and I were at the small airstrip getting ready to catch the single-engine plane to take us across the island. Aibi was there too, to take the same flight. I asked her if I could record the song she had shared earlier in the weekend, so we walked out to the field behind the airstrip and sang. We sang into the tape player, stumbled on the words, laughed and cried together in the tropical sun.

> *May the work that we share speak for us.*
> *And if we fall short of our goal,*
> *Someone come and take ahold.*
> *May the work that we share speak for us.*
> *May the love that we share speak for us*
> *And if we fall short of our goal*
> *Someone come and take ahold.*
> (Source unknown)

## Dare We Open the Screen Door?

I've taught preschool children for 34 years, 31 of which I worked with the Minneapolis Early Childhood Special Education (ECSE) program. Of the more than 80 ECSE staff I worked with, 6 were people of color.

The staff at PICA (Parents in Community Action) Head Start, where we served some of our children, is very diverse and reflects the cultures of the children it serves: Hispanic, Somali, Hmong, African American, and other cultures from Africa and Asia. I'm sure it adds a level of comfort for the children and families to have staff with similar backgrounds as themselves. I longed for that diversity within our Minneapolis school staff.

Our ECSE staff grows more culturally sensitive in their work the longer they are in the field. But why are we not discussing race and class issues that come up in our work? Do teachers and other professionals feel they are not allowed to make mistakes nor ask for help for fear of looking bad or less professional? My 30-plus years of teaching say this is true. This is part of the culture of schools. I felt I should be able to handle whatever came my way and not need to ask for help. For sure, I should be competent to work with all children and all families.

For the past few years, the Minneapolis ECSE program has hired a family therapist who also has experience with children and school staffs to work with our staff. After taking time to build the trust it takes to share in that way, we have begun to discuss issues that arise for us in working closely with parents and school staff. She has coached us on healthier ways to interact with the adults and to remember that we are making a difference in the life of each child, even when we fail to feel it.

## Mistakes Out of Fear

Racism can work in many ways. It can put a person up as well as down. A Native American boy I served who was obese and not very motivated to learn is a case in point. When I did a home visit, I went with thoughts that a Native American family has better values about family than White people, that their reverence and gentleness was healthier than the dominant society's.

What I actually saw I tried not to see or react to, and not to address because of my preconceived ideas. I had seen his siblings making fun of him and teasing him about his eating too much as well as babying him. After the visit, I realized that he was a scapegoat in his family, but I did not address it or suggest ways the other children could be positive with him.

With some African American families where I saw dysfunctional interactions with the child, I did not want to criticize, or to suggest alternative ways they could interact with the child, except by modeling with my interactions. I would often do the same thing with assistants in my classroom. I hoped they would see a different way by observing my interactions. Over the years, I began to realize that this did not work. But I was too afraid to say what I wanted them to do: what was appropriate and healthy for the child and for the atmosphere of the whole classroom.

Sometimes, when my African American boys were out of control and it was time for speech lesson, I relied on the African American speech clinician to bring things under control. They would listen to her stern voice and threats. I did not intervene, but was relieved when the boys' negative behavior stopped.

When I came into one particular Head Start classroom to serve an ECSE child who was very behaviorally challenged, the African American assistant teacher would also gain control in the room by yelling and threatening. I did not feel it was my place to call her on her approach. I knew the director's office was just across the hall, so she must have heard the yelling frequently. I was surprised that this African American director did nothing about it. I regret that I never talked to her about my concerns.

There were also limited positive interactions in this room between the staff and the children. I tried to think of ways to increase interactions and brought games that we could each use with a small group, suggesting that we give positive encouragement for social interaction between the children. I hoped that my role modeling would influence the other teachers. I realized after several months that this approach was ineffective for change.

In another classroom, the teacher let the children "work out" their conflicts on their own, with no intervention by the adults. I never had a dialogue with her about how the child I was serving needed intervention to learn how to interact. She spoke about her philosophy when we met in meetings with parents, but I could see how it played out in the classroom. The only way I attempted to address this was, again, by role modeling when I was in the classroom once each week. Again, no one was watching.

My hope is that young teachers don't wait for retirement, as I did, to bring up these issues. When I speak up now it is in retrospect, in retirement, from the safety of my chair. Do not wait. Do not be afraid. Seek help from your administration and staff. It is for the good of the children that we speak and act.

There were positive outcomes that came out of my relationships with children. Makeel had been placed in a typical preschool classroom, and I saw him once a week as his special education support person. Makeel was an African American boy who was very quiet and withdrawn and, in this preschool, didn't interact with the other children for many months. My work was focused on facilitating his interactions and his enjoyment of being with other children.

When he did begin to open up, he was aggressive with other children. I made home visits when school was not in session and saw how he was with his slightly older brother. His brother was very aggressive toward him. He had learned to defend himself from his brother, and that involved having to fight back. This was very helpful to find out and enabled us to be more realistic in helping him learn social skills and in helping his mother with the interactions between the boys.

Mohamed was a Somali child with autism. His parents showed much affection toward him and loved him as he was. It took a year of weekly visits to help his parents accept this diagnosis and to accept that he needed more help than a home visit could offer. They did enroll him in an autism classroom. Some of the children in that room were severely autistic and aggressive. Mohamed began imitating this behavior at home. One action he imitated was jumping off things, and he broke his arm jumping from a landing in their apartment. They withdrew him from special education and enrolled him in a regular preschool, then in a Minneapolis High Five classroom, from which he was asked to leave, then in Head Start. He had great difficulty in these situations.

In Head Start Mohamed would wander the classroom, not understanding much of what was being said. He was teased by the other Somali children and was not able to form relationships or have conversations with them. Head Start referred him to ECSE, and I was able to see him again and reconnect with the parents. They were accepting of the help; they just didn't want him in an autism classroom. At their request we went through the process of enrolling him in a regular kindergarten for the following year. After two weeks there in the fall, they willingly transferred him to an autism kindergarten. This program worked to integrate the children with special needs into the regular kindergarten as much as the child could handle, with the help of an assistant. This really fit for Mohamed. His parents were very pleased with his progress and wanted him to continue in this program. It took three years to get to know the family, develop a trusting relationship, seek them out after they withdrew Mohamed from special education, and remain available to help them work through the educational system to finally get the appropriate services for Mohamed.

So how did my personal life affect my teaching practice of 31 years? There were parts of it that didn't translate. What kept me silent about the most visible demographic of my workplace? Why did I not talk about the dynamics of being a White working-class woman working with low-income children of color? I was complicit in the silence of schools, where we wouldn't say the "R" word for fear of standing out, making mistakes, being called the "ist" word. I felt fear of being judged, being vulnerable, being not right, and let that fear and shame be stronger than my courage.

As a White ECSE teacher, I entered homes of Somali, Hispanic, and African American families, many lacking resources. I came looking like the social worker or officer that they don't want to see, and yet I expected them to trust me and take my advice. Questions I asked myself:

> Am I careful about the vocabulary of special education so it doesn't put them off? Do I meet them where they are?

Do I provide useful help with skills the child can use each day, skills that really help the parent meet the child's needs? Do I do it in a way that is enjoyable?

Naturally, I made judgments when I walked in. *Why is this child not the focus of this family? Why are there no toys and children's books for these children? Why don't they allow the children outside to play? Why is the TV on all the time? Why doesn't the parent want to play with us? Don't they know the language and behavior they use in front of the child will be imitated by the child?!*

It is always easier when the parents or guardians welcome me in and are attentive to their child. It's easier when there aren't other adults around distracting the child or parent. It's easier when the house is orderly and quiet. But how do I do my work when it's not?

We are trained to know child development and the answers to the children's problems. But we are not trained to be a facilitator, a coach, a trainer of caregivers. Diversity training often involves knowledge about the cultures but not about the interactions. In our society where the poor communities of color are isolated, there is little chance for everyday interactions across the color divide. How do I bridge that gap?

How do I get beyond my guilt as a White person to be authentic in my interactions with them? If my focus is to empower parents to be their child's primary teacher, as they are, how do I approach them? Is my need to be accepted keeping me from having expectations of the parents, that they will follow through with teaching skills to their child?

What is our mental framework when we begin this sensitive work? Has our teacher training opened our eyes to societal prejudices? Do we go in with some pity and condescension as well as our good intentions and knowledge?

Do we teach only from the knowledge we've learned, or do we incorporate the family lifestyle and culture into a cooperative dance, teaching and learning for us as well as them?

I have many questions to help the dialogue begin.

## Journal Questions

1. Nancy says in her writing, "Why did I not talk about my Polish and Swedish heritage and make it as prominent as the African American side of our family?" In your journal, flow write an answer to Nancy's question to herself: Guess, pretend, fabricate, lie, but have fun.

2. Think about an experience when you felt humiliated like Nancy did in an incident with her Black roommate. In your journal write the line, "Why did I not say something then—or ever—about the incident?" Flow write an answer to the question.

3. In your journal take a line or two from Nancy's poem "Friendship with a Black woman / Crossing the color line . . ." and use the line(s) as the beginning of your own poem.

4. In your journal, flow write an answer to this question from Nancy's story: "Why do Caucasians always have to own/put their stamp on everything?" Write with feeling. Let the sadness, anger, hopelessness, and/or frustration flow through your pen.

5. Write the following statements in your journal, filling in the blanks. Write, write, write.

Culture is dynamic, so to say something is continuously culturally appropriate is _____. The lies we tell ourselves about culture when we don't criticize _____ behavior are _____.

List examples of cultural referents you know about.

*Peggy Semingson in 2011*

7

# "SABER DOS LENGUAS ES SABER DOS MUNDOS"

Thoughts From a
White Bilingual Educator

*Peggy Semingson*

"I started to think about voice. Whose voice prevailed in the classroom? . . . It was only during this year that I was truly able to transform the curriculum into something more meaningful that connected to my students' lives."

I grew up in the northern wastelands of Alaska, surrounded by wilderness but also great cultural richness and diversity among the people. Although I was White and had been born in Austin, Texas, my first 10 years were spent immersed in a setting of Native Alaskan values and culture in Kodiak Island, Fairbanks, North Pole, and Anchorage. My twin sister and I grew up in Alaska during the Reagan-Thatcher cold war years in the 1980s, somewhat isolated from the "lower 48," as we called it, and were rough-and-tough, proud, and very independent.

Alaska women, for instance, did not conform to traditional gender roles. There was a kind of "communal living" sense always present in Alaska, and reciprocity was a shared value. We showered at my aunt's house. At home our water came from a nearby creek, or we hauled it back in huge jugs from the local fire station. My grandma did my uncle's laundry and sewed his clothes. My uncle, in turn, did car repair for everyone, and as small children, we helped with laundry on Saturdays at the laundromat on the military base. I had a glimpse into a temporary poverty that I would always remember, but it was just that—temporary.

Geographically, Alaska was like a foreign country. I remember hearing when I was small about the "United States" and I didn't know if I lived in it. I knew I lived in the far north. I knew I was surrounded by Native Alaskan culture, language, food, and customs. I wasn't even sure whether I was even an American until I came to realize the geography and appreciate the odd fact that Alaska is, indeed, part of the United States. Although we were White, many White Alaskans also greatly appreciated and admired the traditions of Native Alaskans.

In 1984, when I was 10, my family relocated from Alaska when my stepfather took a job in San Diego. In the contrasting environment of Southern California, my journey changed from feeling like a foreigner to becoming a "Valley girl." We lived in a middle-class condo community in the suburbs of San Diego, and the little I knew about the Latino experience came from my high school Spanish classes, where we mainly read literature from Spain—not Mexico—despite being 15 miles from the United States–Mexico border crossing. However, it was in my high school Spanish class that I became proficient enough in the language to later become certified as a bilingual elementary teacher in Texas. It was here that Mr. Mora, our Spanish teacher, told us repeatedly, "Saber dos lenguas es saber dos mundos," meaning "To know two languages is to know two worlds." Although I understood this intellectually, I feel as though I spent the next 20 years attempting to live it—sometimes successfully, but sometimes not. Although I knew I was culturally aware and sensitive from my early years in diverse settings, I always struggled to present myself as a cultural insider when I clearly was not.

## Southern California Teaching Years: Carpinteria and Fallbrook

I remember my first year teaching at Aliso Elementary School in Carpinteria, California, in the context of the predominantly English instruction that had taken over the state. The year was 1997. Because of the recent passage of Proposition 227, English for the Children, Spanish was essentially eliminated from the curriculum and classrooms across the state, replaced by a curriculum that emphasized mostly English instruction. Technically, the rules permitted some amount of Spanish to be spoken in the classroom, but in actuality I, and perhaps others, wondered whether there would be an unknown penalty for doing so. Implicitly it was understood that primarily English was to be spoken. Ironically, it was in this context that my journey as a bilingual educator began.

My first year teaching fifth grade, predominantly "English only," I had many students who were Latino English language learners. My knowledge of how to engage and teach my Latino students was limited to my knowledge of the language, interactions with childhood friends, and to some extent, what I learned from student teaching at the same school. The curriculum I chose for the students hardly reflected their culture, values, beliefs, or linguistic heritage. We read Newbery Medal–winning books—books that were considered quality literature but at that time did little to value the cultural and linguistic "funds of knowledge" that Luis Moll and colleagues (Moll & González, 2004) discuss in their research connecting home and school learning.

Two events opened my eyes that year to the ways that I, the *maestra*, had a powerful role to play as gatekeeper of learning and of our shared classroom space. My second year teaching in the same coastal California town of Carpinteria, a small agricultural community just south of the resort town of Santa Barbara, I was invited by one of my students to come visit his home.

Third grader Leonel (all names are pseudonyms), a bilingual learner, invited me to visit his family across the street from the school. Almost daily, it seemed, he insisted I come over to meet his family. At first, I wondered if his requests were idle conversation. After several insistent invitations from him and one from his mother, I made the short trip to where they lived. My Spanish was rusty, but I was grateful for the opportunity to converse in a language that was a comfort to many of the children I worked with.

Leonel's mother remarked that my Spanish was "good." She asked me about my childhood in Alaska and *did my family work in the fields*. I had a moment of cognitive dissonance. Did she know I was White? Was I White in her eyes? What did that mean if I wasn't? Did she think I came from a family of Latino immigrants? I did not ask my questions.

We had dinner, talked about school and their family routines, and I admired her interest in and dedication to her child's education. It was my first home visit, and I wished I could say I initiated it, but I didn't. This one visit opened my eyes to my students' lives outside of the classroom. The next day Leonel boasted to his third-grade companions, "The *maestra* came to my house!"

Why hadn't I done that sooner? I began to seek out ways to connect with the students' lives. I came to know and communicate with the parents and families through phone calls and invitations for them to visit the classroom, mainly to request their help in a volunteer capacity or for parent conferences. However, I never ventured into homes again; it was outside my comfort zone.

Another significant visit took place in my third-grade classroom that same school year that shaped my thinking and beliefs. Marisol was a recent immigrant from Mexico. She spoke predominantly Spanish. A fiercely hardworking student, she worked her way through the not-so-culturally-relevant curriculum of my classroom. I admired her tenacity, her desire to learn English, and her perfect Spanish when we tried to communicate with one another.

One afternoon, in a quiet empty classroom at the end of the day, Marisol's parents came in unannounced. Her dad was an agricultural worker and came in with his wife after work to talk to me. His demeanor was serious and so was his message. "*Maestra*," he began. He proceeded to tell me in Spanish that he and his wife had not completed their education in Mexico. "*No sabemos nada. Todo lo que aprende Marisol, ella tiene que aprender de usted.*" They told me, "Teacher, we don't know anything. Everything Marisol learns, she has to learn from you." These powerful words floored me. Was it true they "knew nothing"? Were his words intentionally made to be dramatic so I would pay extra attention to his daughter? I had never experienced a parent telling me such a thing, nor could I imagine my own mother saying these words to a teacher. This father let his voice be heard and let me know the power of education, and the positioning of teacher-as-expert, and my role in educating his daughter. This memory haunted me the rest of my teaching career and to this day.

When I began teaching, it was from my own school-centered perspective; I assumed that I had the "expertise" of a university-trained teacher—knowledge that needed to be shared to those that I perceived to be less-knowing others. Today I see this kind of thinking reflects a deficient way of viewing parents. I had known the perspectives of parents only in a very limited way: from my mainstream, White, middle-class female perspective.

It is necessary to seek information from parents themselves on their perspectives and needs rather than to make assumptions about what we think they need, know, or don't know. My realization about the need to listen to parents, hear their voices, and value their cultures and home literacy practices began at Aliso Elementary School.

A final turning point took place while I was working in California. In 1997 I attended the conference of the California Association of Bilingual Education. It was months before Proposition 227 dealt its heavy blow of "English only." Educators openly cried, we discussed curriculum possibilities, and I attended a session by some researchers from UC Berkeley advocating the use of the theoretical framework of *Funds of Knowledge*, designed by Luis Moll and colleagues (Moll & González, 2004) at the University of Arizona. The framework calls for educators to value students' cultural and linguistic resources from the home and community. I sat and wondered for a really long time what this might mean for my classroom.

I was fascinated by the idea of tapping into strengths and assets that students brought, but I struggled to connect theory to practice. I left the conference resenting the "ivory tower" folks who just didn't know what the classroom was like.

## Deep in the Heart of Texas: A Bilingual Teacher, Finally

After teaching for three years in Carpinteria, I left California and moved to Texas in search of a lower cost of living. I moved back to my roots, to my birthplace, Austin. Not only was I able to reconnect with extended family, but I was able to seek certification to become a bilingual teacher in a state that offered a variety of bilingual programs.

I felt better about myself: The state had authorized me to teach in the students' native language. At the same time, I was scared and excited. Questions raced through my mind. Was my Spanish good enough? Would I be able to communicate my own ideas? What did it mean to be a White teacher teaching in a language that wasn't my own? I had no friends, no community, yet. I desperately wanted to be responsible to the students, to provide them the best education that I could.

### *The Beginning of Transformation*

I taught in a small suburban district in central Texas, in a dual language fifth-grade classroom, again with all Caucasian and Latino students. The Latino students' parents in my class were largely working-class. Four of my students were recent immigrants from Mexico and spoke mostly Spanish. In this fourth year of teaching, I began to think about the idea of "funds of knowledge" again and how I could possibly use it in my classroom.

I was given the opportunity to implement an informal action research project in my classroom, and I decided to intentionally design my yearlong project as a reading-writing workshop in which students would write about their lives and experiences. I requested book sets full of titles that would connect to their culture and language. I had recently seen a movie based on Tomás Rivera's memoir-like novel *Y no se lo trajo la tierra/ . . . And the Earth Did Not Devour Him* (1987). I bought a set of the Rivera novels for the students. I bought more bilingual books from Cinco Puntos Press—stories about La Llorona and other folklore tales that built on the students' oral language.

I connected back to what I had learned in my one class in Chicano Studies at the University of California, Santa Barbara. That class, along with my language learning in high school and my living in the borderlands of San Diego, was most of what I knew about Latino culture. Thankfully, my students also taught me. They gently corrected my grammatical mistakes uttered in Spanish. Because the word order, or syntax, is different in Spanish than in English, I would sometimes mix up the order of my words, and even though they understood me, they would repeat back what I had intended to say in the correct way, as if leading the instruction—something I was "supposed" to do. They, in turn, devoured the bilingual and culturally relevant books. They asked for more and suggested titles and authors I had never heard of. I read along with them and discussed Latino and Chicano literature at parent conferences with the Spanish-speaking parents and sought their perspectives.

In the four walls of my classroom that first year in Texas, the students lined the bulletin boards with their written narratives and pictures. They interviewed family members about their life stories and expertise and wrote about it. They shared with the class stories of migration and of living in border towns.

I learned about Eagle Pass, San Antonio, mobility, and trips to Dallas to see a large extended family. Their narratives were new to me. I was constantly comparing their experiences to my own memories, always learning from them and wanting to know more about their lives. Daily, our class routine incorporated "Sharing Time," during which students felt safe to share not things but stories. I valued their experiences and their voices.

I started to think about voice. Whose voice prevailed in the classroom? Where was my voice, my students' voices, their cultural voice, how did they line up? It was only during this year that I was truly able to transform the curriculum into something more meaningful that connected to my students' lives. When I did my student teaching, the curriculum was all about me and what I knew. The students read Jack London's *The Call of the Wild* and I "informed" them about Alaskan values. Now, years later, I was finally learning to listen instead of talk. I was learning about reciprocity in listening and sharing.

As I continued to teach, as a classroom teacher and eventually as a bilingual reading specialist in Texas, I continued to develop meaning making and sharing of voice throughout the literacy curriculum, especially during writing workshop. While I pursued a master's degree and doctorate in literacy, and as I continued my work as a bilingual classroom teacher and later as a bilingual reading specialist, I started to focus on two features of connecting literacy learning to my students' backgrounds and knowledge. I took charge of the curriculum in the classroom and made it more accessible and beneficial to the students, all the while receiving little direct instruction or support from the school. Most of what I learned about my students' culture and lives, I learned on my own time and also from the students themselves.

The first aspect of this intentional curricular change was the incorporation of bilingual books into the classroom. I had a lot to learn about this topic. I spoke the language reasonably well, but I had little insight into what it meant to *be* Latino. I had to educate myself. I went back in my mind to the Chicano studies class and what I had learned there. I remembered learning about Alma Flor Ada, a Latina activist and prolific children's book writer. I attended literacy conferences such as the Texas Association of Bilingual Education and sought out workshops on culturally relevant teaching.

The second aspect was the creation and nurturing of a true writer's workshop where students self-selected topics that mattered to them and created powerful writing pieces representing their own voice and experiences.

My eighth year teaching in the classroom, I used Carmen Lomas Garza's picture books *Family Pictures/Cuadros de Familia* (1990) and *In My Family/En Mi Familia* (1996) as central, touchstone texts to build on. The students could relate to much of what they read and saw in the author's realistic vignettes and artwork based on her own life as a Chicana Texan. I deliberately used the comprehension strategy of "making connections" (Harvey & Goudvis, 2007) by connecting the author's ideas to the students' own background knowledge and experiences. I asked them, "Have you been to a fair like this? What was it like? What did you do? Who went with you? Let's talk about it." Our conversation was as much for the students' self-expression as it was a learning experience for me.

Students brought in photos of significant moments in their life, examined them closely with magnifying glasses, and shared the details of their stories. We celebrated these photo essays often. They wrote about these pictures of family, ordinary lives, and celebrations. We made books in both English and Spanish. Again, the walls of the classroom were lined with their voices and tales. We enjoyed reading each others' stories. We had author's chair. I invited parents into the classroom to participate in the sharing of stories. At the beginning of the year and throughout the year, I asked the parents their hopes and dreams for their children. They told me of their great aspirations for their children.

### *"You Are a Book"*

At the same time we were engaging in these culturally meaningful conversations, I was surrounded by the pervasive milieu of pressure being created by imposed standardized testing. I felt the tensions and the expectations. It got to me. I allowed "teaching to the test" to take priority over cultural relevance. It was stressful, and at the center of my mind was the thought that, for the student, passing or failing a high-stakes test meant proceeding to the next grade or being retained.

However, I did find time to continue the writer's workshop. I often modeled my own writing on chart paper in front of the students. I hoped to inspire my students with tales of living in Alaska, adventures with my twin sister, and other Wild North experiences and events. I was open and honest with them and understood my limitations and my experiences as a White woman who happened to know their language, also in a limited way.

One day, Araceli approached my desk as I was about to distribute one of the often-given "benchmark" tests that would quantify their writing abilities into a single score. Araceli looked me in the eye and, locked onto my gaze, informed me, "Ms. Semingson, you are a book." She caught me off guard and I was quite puzzled.

"What do you mean?" I replied, the researcher in me wanting to know more.

"Because you're always telling us stories," she said matter-of-factly.

"What stories are those, Araceli?" I inquired.

"The stories of your life," she answered, never losing my gaze.

I had stories that sometimes paralleled the themes of their lives, but more often I didn't. I knew what I shared of myself made an impact on how they formed their own personal narratives—narratives that would construct their identity in words and writing. Some of the students wanted to be like me; they saw me as a model but weren't quite sure what to make of me.

Third-grader Benita wasn't sure of my identity and shared in an essay, "When I grow up I want to be a Chicana like Ms. Semingson, whose Spanish is not so good." Josue, who greatly loved school and disliked vacations because they meant less learning, told me—even though I knew he was from Mexico—he, too, had a twin and his twin still lived in Alaska! What I shared of myself, including my identity as White woman, impacted their own identities.

I did share commonalities with my students; we shared both language and common stories and experiences. Many of us White teachers will not *ever* be within a nondominant culture, but we can enter it, interact within it as I have done as a bilingual educator, encourage the sharing of its voices, and for a time and in shared space, together appreciate both our commonalities and our differences. I loved being in the classroom with children who brought rich and complex cultural and linguistic resources to the room with them. I wanted to always remember the voice of Benita and the images and words—in both English and Spanish—of all of their photo essays, and I knew I needed to go back to school in order to honor their voices.

## Education Requires Active Involvement by All Parties

I am now living in the Dallas–Fort Worth Metroplex area after finishing graduate studies at the University of Texas at Austin. My dissertation, a series of home visits and interviews with parents in a low-income community in a large city in Texas, focused on the perspective of parents about their children's literacy learning (Semingson, 2008). I knew from my years in the classroom, and from that first visit to Leonel's house in Carpinteria, that I needed to make more in-depth home visits and listen to parents and families. It took eight years for me to finally intentionally visit and interview parents from a low-income community. And I did hear their voices speaking out, loud and clear, letting me know they had a story to tell.

I approached parents I barely knew and invited myself into their homes. In doing these home visits, I also saw a side of the families that allowed me to see the "whole child" and to gain insight into the day-to-day life of the children I knew in a school context. I was greatly humbled by the stories the parents chose to share with me. I saw the multifaceted, creative, and mutually beneficial ways that families support one another's literacy and language experiences in the home. I saw that this supportive environment was rooted in the parents' caring and concern for their children. The parents were essential partners that I had not often reached out to in active ways and *were experts that I had ignored.* Looking back, the few parents I connected with—and learned from—had reached out to me first. How could I have forgotten parents in the student/teacher equation? Why didn't I attempt to build that relationship as well, and not wait until a parent came forward first? The realization that I had neglected to be proactive in seeking out the knowledge and support of the family of the children I taught was a crushing blow to my ideas about myself as an educator. Why had it taken me so long to reach out to families? Did having privilege stop me?

Visiting the homes made me more sensitized to the families. I now think of the complex stories the parents told me and how their stories are bound together with mine. I now carry their stories around in my head and heart and recall their words and voices telling me of life successes, challenges, and goals. I can hear their distinct voices, their enunciation of emotionally laden statements about the school's distrust of them. For over a year, I could hear Alejandra fully describing her daughter's ways of learning and the strengths that her daughter brought to bear on academic tasks like homework and reading. She proudly shared with me stories of success and many affirming statements about her daughter. I took these statements with me and wrote about them in several articles so that I could share their stories with educators.

I connected what I learned from visiting the families to my daily classroom learning—putting "theory" into practice in a meaningful way. I now know from my interviews and observations that many children read together in social and collaborative ways. In my elementary classroom, during our daily independent reading time, I observed the behavior of the bilingual, working-class third graders. They often preferred to read together in pairs or small groups. My efforts to get them to read totally individually were often met with subtle and overt resistance. They inevitably formed small groups anyway, and I "gave in" and went back to partner reading. Because I had such a variety of high-interest text, while reading alone they would often hold up the book and display an interesting picture across the room, making their literacy practices social. By allowing the students this space to share and collaborate in ways they knew, using their home and cultural ways of speaking and communicating, I fostered an environment in which students participated more successfully in the classroom.

I currently conduct research with Latina mothers, seeking their perspectives on their children's literacy learning. I draw largely on narrative methods. I value their voices. No voice should be silenced, but so often they are, including our own. In my current research, I am often aware of my outsider status. Recently, I taught a library-sponsored family literacy workshop in a predominantly Latino apartment community in Spanish. At first, the mothers didn't know I spoke Spanish and were relieved to find out I knew their language. During the workshop, I was there to educate them about literacy learning in the home. However, I became painfully aware that I knew very little of the literacy events, culture, and experiences that children who come from Latin American countries are immersed in. I still had little understanding of the rich background of cultural experiences the mothers shared with their children in the household. For instance, the mothers told me about the entertainer "Cri Cri." "Who is Cri Cri?" I asked a Latina colleague. "Cri Cri . . . is Cri Cri," she attempted to explain to me. Over the years I came to the realization that I need to know more about their lives; I only knew my own.

I had so much to learn, and as a classroom teacher I often felt like there was so little time to get to know parents and families in the school context. On the parent-teacher conference day, we were allotted 15 minutes for each parent. Often working parents are not able to come to school during the day, or might be limited by transportation or other constraints, so many times the conferences were lined up back-to-back, double booked in a sense, in case a parent was a "no-show." The back-to-back nature of the conferences and the fact that they take place only once or twice a year seems to limit and systematically constrain dialogue and open communication. There is often little time whatsoever to hear about the parents' lives or seek insight from them about their son or daughter.

Often I was given a one-page sheet with formal school data such as standardized testing information and was required to share that data with parents. Although I had other things to share with parents, or inquire of them, there was very little time within the 15-minute conference to ask the parents anything. I wonder whether the parents felt similarly, like there was no time to question me or dialogue about their child.

My journey as a bilingual educator began with my determined study of Spanish in high school, during my formative years in the diverse setting of Alaska. My learning is a sine wave with peaks and valleys that alternate between thinking I know a lot and then realizing I know very little. I am often bumped up against situations in which I feel ignorant and humbled by how little I know about race, class, gender, or what it means to be part of a bilingual community. I continue learning and growing so I can become a better teacher who helps other teachers work with children from diverse backgrounds.

Growing up with the beauty of Alaska's vast terrain, beautiful mountains, fumaroles, and river basins, I realize the diversity of land left me with a deep awe of difference. And today I carry that geography with me, but instead of water and earth it is the depth of linguistic and cultural assets that students bring to the classroom, an immeasurable landscape of experiences and knowledge that I encourage teachers to build their literacy curriculum on. Despite the learning and transformation that came about through my interactions with the children and families, I realize that, like my journeys into Alaska's geography 1,480 miles long and 810 miles wide, my journey to understand diverse populations has covered very little ground, and I have mountaintops and valleys yet to explore.

## Journal Questions

1. In your journal, first flow write a reaction to the story (see "Journaling" in the introduction of this book for a description of flow writing). If you underlined words that "spoke" to you as you read, write from those as well.

2. Peggy saw herself in an "outsider status." Have you ever felt in that position, in your family, work, or social group? Write about what it was like for you. Are there advantages as well as discomfort in this perspective?

3. As a teacher or teacher in training, have you learned things from your students' life stories or artwork that have given you insight into your teaching practice? That have influenced what you do? Write about it, trying to get out of the realm of theory and into the concrete and practical.

4. Peggy had a "transformation" in her teaching experience. If you have had such an experience, journal about it. If not, what do you imagine could move you to such an experience? Create a vision of such a scenario (for example, imagine having the support you need—maybe two teachers per room—having trust among staff to share mistakes, and so on).

## References

Garza, C. L. (1990). *Family pictures/Cuadros de familia.* San Francisco: Children's Book Press.

Garza, C. L. (1996). *In my family/En mi familia.* San Francisco: Children's Book Press.

Harvey, S., & Goudvis, A. (2007). *Strategies that work: Teaching for understanding and engagement* (2nd ed.). Portland, ME: Stenhouse Publishers.

Moll, L. C., & González, N. (2004). Engaging life: A funds-of-knowledge approach to multicultural education. In J. Banks & C. McGee Banks (Eds.), *Handbook of research on multicultural education* (2nd ed., pp. 699–715). San Francisco: Jossey-Bass.

Rivera, T. (1987). *Y no se lo trago la tierra (And the earth did not devour him)* (E. Vigil-Piñón, Trans.). Houston, TX: Arte Público Press.

Semingson, P. (2008). "O.K., Let's figure it out all together": Parents' narratives about their children's literacy learning in the home and school. Unpublished doctoral dissertation, The University of Texas at Austin, Austin, TX.

Tara L. Affolter

# 8

# PIANO LESSONS

## A White Teacher Struggles to Share the Spotlight

*Tara L. Affolter*

"We were together; we were united in our dislike of the White man's destruction of the Ibo culture. I clearly got it. I was so proud. That is, until a student named Michael pushed me to see a bit more. 'You may be a nice lady. You may even talk about justice, but I will never trust you because you are White.'"

Despite the assertion that American society is becoming postracial, we can look at many schools across our nation and realize that we are still living in a White-dominated world that only masquerades as a color-blind place. Theater programs provide a remarkable opportunity to view a microcosm of this larger masquerade. As a high school English and theater teacher I learned to struggle against practicing color blindness, but that learning was slow, painful, and demanding of me in ways I had never imagined. I am convinced, though, that it is only through this process of working and growing with my students that I moved further in my own anti-racist stance.

I originally entered teaching with a deep desire to disrupt inequities in schools. I had grown up in an overtly racist town, but my family frequently discussed the unacceptable nature of racism. My parents taught us to reject explicit and overt examples of racism—"we don't use those words," "we don't treat people that way"—simple, direct, and powerfully fundamental to who I am. However, given that I was brought up in an all-White town by parents who grew up in that same town, my understanding of racism was extremely limited. Thus, I grew up believing in a color-blind ideal even though I had no words for it at the time.

I like to think that as I entered teaching I had a more complex understanding of race and racism, but in examining my first choices as a theater director it is clear that I did not. I did immediately focus on dealing with racism, and as a new teacher at Central High School in Champaign, Illinois. I first chose to stage an adaption of Harper Lee's *To Kill a Mockingbird*. This was my favorite book and film as a child. Atticus was my hero, and I felt excited to bring this story to the stage and proud to include African American students who had not previously had much to do with this school's theater program. It was a start, but looking back on it I can clearly see the imprint of my early learning on these choices.

The focus of *To Kill a Mockingbird* is on good White people like Atticus Finch; the main Black characters are Tom Robinson, the victim of a racist system, and Calpurnia, who is never fully a member of the Finch family. I never talked about these lessons with my students because I didn't understand them for a while. It seemed enough to have students on stage together, but I would soon learn that it was not nearly enough.

In addition to my job as a theater director at Central High I was an English teacher there. As a new teacher I was assigned to lower level classes, which in this school were made up of predominantly African American students. I was frustrated by the low expectations for these students and the lack of materials provided for the course. I felt that my frustration and my solidarity with the inequity I was witnessing was enough.

By the spring of my first year, I had won a small battle within the English department and was given permission to teach Chinua Achebe's *Things Fall Apart* to my "low" 10th-grade English class. So here we were, dissecting colonialism in Nigeria and discussing issues of justice. We were together; we were united in our dislike of the White man's destruction of the Ibo culture. I clearly got it. I was so proud. That is, until a student named Michael pushed me to see a bit more. "You may be a nice lady. You may even talk about justice, but I will never trust you because you are White."

My face flushed and I blinked back tears before I was literally saved by the bell. That night, despite crying jags and rambling on about how the student "didn't even know me," a few seeds of change were planted in me. However, it would take some time before I could accept how my own skin granted me privilege that Michael could never access.

## Classtime

Another one of my classes was pushing me to learn, too. This one was also predominantly Black, with the added twist of being almost completely composed of 10th-grade girls. Three of the 15 girls were pregnant, one for the second time. I felt little connection with these young women, and they surely didn't need another "nice White teacher" being kind to them but not teaching. They didn't need a teacher who didn't know what do when ultra-sound pictures were passed around. They needed someone to teach them, and that person was not me—at least not yet.

One day, somewhere around Martin Luther King Jr.'s birthday, I began quoting Dr. King. I was working myself into a frenzy of peace and justice when I was interrupted by Faith, who rarely spoke. "That man is dead. They shot him." "But look around," I thought (and may have said). "Things have changed." And then I looked around and thought about the way this school not only tracked students into high-, medium-, and low-level classes but also weighted the grades in each track so that an A in the low-level English class was not worth as much as an A in another class. I thought about the way that argument extended to the poor treatment the students in the class received within the school and within our community, and I painfully real-ized that the students were quantified in much the same way as their grades were in the course hierarchy. They didn't count as much as the (White) students in higher tracks.

For a while this outrage fueled me in narrow but temporarily empower-ing ways. I demanded our little class be given the same grade points afforded to the higher track. I brought up the tracking problem at nearly every depart-ment meeting. I spoke with the Office of Civil Rights that was investigating our district for various violations including this tracking debacle. I wanted to change the school, but at this point, even though I didn't know it at the time, I was working largely from a White savior position. "Look at me doing these good things for these students, especially all these poor, Black young women. I am good. Hear me roar."

## Time for a Change

This brings me back to my role as the theater director. During my first year I felt rather proud of my productions of *To Kill a Mockingbird* and *A Mid-summer Night's Dream* (complete with an African American female playing Puck and an African American male as Oberon). To my thinking, I had made some inroads toward creating a more inclusive community. I felt my work countered the hostile nature of the school toward African American students and the overtly racist practices I witnessed. I was confident that I provided a safe space for students of color. To some degree it was true, but it was only by my sifting through these issues and allowing myself to learn that a more fundamental shift took place within me.

For the next several years my teaching career followed this story line. I grew as an anti-racist educator and as a person, and the English department and my theater program made incremental progress toward serving Black students in more meaningful and equitable ways. And then, as I was milling outside the gym after a school pep rally, an incident took place that shook me enough to try something more radical.

School had just let out, and students were streaming out to greet the weekend when a police car pulled into the circle driveway. Before I fully understood what was happening, Terrell, a starting basketball player, was being handcuffed and led to the car. The students around me froze. Terrell avoided eye contact. I overheard another Black student say, "There goes another n*****." There was silence as students watched and shook their heads. I wanted to fill the silence with something else. I shifted that day and have been shifting ever since.

Auditions for the next play were coming up, and I made the decision to direct an all-Black play by August Wilson entitled *The Piano Lesson*. The late August Wilson's significant legacy is a 10-play cycle depicting aspects of African American experiences in the twentieth century, each play set in a different decade. *The Piano Lesson* is the fourth play in the cycle. As a college student I had admired Wilson's work but had never really considered staging one of these plays at a high school. I was excited and intimidated by the prospect of taking this next step and felt it was the right thing to do for our school, which was in so many ways failing to provide an equitable education for all students.

To say the process was transformative somehow diminishes what it meant to me and to my students. In preparing to write this chapter I contacted some of the students from my cast of *The Piano Lesson* and asked them about what being in the play meant. Although forever frozen as teenagers in my mind, the students, now in their late 20s and early 30s, continue to teach me years later. Here Tyson describes how being in the play had a lasting impact on him far beyond high school.

> I didn't realize the tremendous impact that being a part of *The Piano Lesson* cast would have on my future decisions and location, but to say the least

it served as a foundation for my internal character . . . from the moment the school saw me on stage as "Boy Willie" I gained my first positive identity at school. I was known for being good at something. For me this was a pivotal point in my life. This is when I noticed I could work hard at something and the visions in my head would come true.

Being involved in *The Piano Lesson* was one of the reasons I petitioned Central High School to add an African American history class. Being involved in the play was one of the reasons I chose to move to Mississippi to further my education, as well as one of the reasons why I will stay here (in Mississippi) to help bring about change to the impoverished conditions that African American people live in down here.

Clearly, when I chose to do the play I had no way of knowing what it would mean to or how it would be received by students or staff. As Kanitra, another original cast member, put it, "I did not know at the time that we were making history, and it still does not seem like we made (history) in the school." We were just doing this play together, and in some small way I was hoping that this was enough to give students who had largely been ignored or marginalized in the school a chance to be seen and heard. But by and large we labored alone, built our community alone, and made this happen *alone.* That a play did not destroy decades of inequitable treatment should not surprise me, but a girl can dream. We didn't transform the school. Yet there was so much learning that happened during the process that it remains significant for me, the students, and perhaps the larger community.

At best, it would be naïve to suggest that merely putting on an August Wilson play is proof that I am/was committed to students of color or that my presence and my work was welcomed and trusted by all. After all, Wilson himself discussed his preference for Black directors for his work. And why not? As a White woman I bring an entirely different understanding to my reading and directing. A task early on was for me to "come clean" with my limitations and to ask the students to allow me to learn with them as we built characters and created understandings of the text.

One way of doing this was to discuss frankly the use of the *n-word,* which Wilson frequently uses throughout his text. In fact, the word is used in the opening sequence of *The Piano Lesson.* Who was I, as a White woman, to ask my Black students to use that term in reference to each other? Despite the fact that I understood that the word meant different things in different contexts, I still felt that under my direction the word might take on a different and unintended meaning.

I considered cutting the *n-word* completely, but then I considered how my own history with the term, my own early teaching, might limit my view. As a cast we discussed my history with the word. Looking back I cringe a bit about the focus on me during this discussion. I was surrounded by young African American students who each had a story to tell. Nonetheless, we started there, and the students slowly weighed in on the discussion.

Some students agreed and expressed a dislike for the word in any context. Others found my nearly visceral response to the word funny. In the end, we used the word where the students felt comfortable as they grew into their characters. The students demonstrated insight far beyond their years in understanding that the audiences (still largely White) might misconstrue the frequent use of the word and miss the richness of the performance.

In the play the students typically substituted for the "n-word" in friendly conversation with "fool" or "boy." But when angry or talking about how Whites treated them, they would choose to have their character use the term. My students understood that White audiences and their White director could never fully understand various alternative readings and uses of the term. Yes, initially the spotlight was on my experiences with the n-word, but gradually I started to learn *with* my students about language and culture and this word. And the transformation began.

I learned more than just language. I learned about hot combs, Mississippi families, Parchment Farm, and chain gangs. I learned about students' histories and families. I learned that their parents knew about this play and it meant something to them. (Kanitra's mom lent us old family photos to help us get the right feel of the time period.) I learned that the cast chose to get a ride home from rehearsal every night together in our paneled minivan (my husband also taught at the school and was a key component in bringing the show to life) even though some of them could get home faster by walking. I later learned that there was an ongoing dispute about whom would be dropped off last, because the cast wanted to stay together as long as possible. As parents hosted a reception for us on opening night, I learned that the community had noticed our labor of love. And as I watched students reenacting scene after scene as the set came down, I learned that this play meant more than the sum of the performances.

Later that spring we staged *The Wiz*, which is an African American take on *The Wizard of Oz*, and although we had a multiracial cast, the impact of not having "whitewashed" the cast was quite clear. Femi, another performer in *The Piano Lesson* as well as *The Wiz*, writes of this:

. . . at first, I only knew to respond to it (*The Piano Lesson*) as I responded to any other play. *The Piano Lesson* just kind of felt like "The Black Play" at first, like we were getting to do a special show just because we were Black. It wasn't until *The Wiz* that I realized my Blackness had a unique impact on the role I was playing. I could speak using my more relaxed dialect, and it helped the part. I could sing the way I was taught in the Black church, and it made the song sound better. And I can't quite remember the sequence of what show I was in after that, but I know that I was resolved to be all of who I was in everything I did from then on. I remember that a teacher once commented that she had heard me talking in the hallway to my friends, and it sounded different than when I talked to her in my class. I was embarrassed by that. Not the case after being in these shows. People actually got to see the complete Femi, know that I was multifaceted, and accept it. Or not.

Ultimately, and ironically, I learned that, although what I did meant something to my students and to the larger school, I could not simply ponder the inequities that my school was replicating. What I was doing didn't feel like enough. I needed a deeper understanding and I needed more tools.

At the close of that school year, I headed off to graduate school at the University of Wisconsin at Madison. Again, Kanitra's words help to frame some of the tension in that choice: "You are one teacher that I will never forget. You made such a heavy impression in my heart, and I was very sad for a long time when you left. But I was happy to share you with others who may have needed you to believe in them as you did us." I read those words and think back on my choice to leave these students right after they had been "seen" by the school for the first time. I realize, again, this isn't a tidy story.

## The Drama Kids

My experiences in my first job (at Central) framed the rest of my work. So when I arrived at graduate school I made the decision to stay in touch with my teaching roots by directing the East High School theater program. Although the town itself was larger and more diverse than Champaign, Illinois, I encountered the same issues. I discovered the theater program that I had inherited at this new school was very White and very closed to newcomers.

My first introduction to the theater kids came when I called a meeting and found five or six students waiting for me in the theater. All White and wearing matching theater T-shirts, the students rushed to meet me because they wanted to speak with me before I spoke with the rest of the students. These were the Drama Kids, who had been afforded significant power by the former director. She allowed everything from skipping classes and joining her for lunch to taking smoking breaks with her. The students were clearly concerned that their privileges were under siege and were attempting to assert control of the theater department.

At the time I was not too rattled. Any new teacher faces at least some students for whom the former teacher was perfect. Yet I was to learn that this selectiveness, this closed society, was not just new-student jitters but a standard mode of operation and community building within the theater program.

Carrying with me the victories and transformations I had gained at Central, I began a campaign to increase student involvement and diversity in the program. I encountered resistance, to say the least. I instituted the practice of double casting (placing two students in each role) to provide more students a chance to perform. This policy, along with my efforts to bring in more students, particularly students of color, was met with silence and doubt. After a year of such resistance, I began to see the exclusive and selective nature of the program as a manifestation of White privilege. I started a small research project to find out how Whiteness was policed and maintained in the theater program and, more important, to force myself to de-center Whiteness and challenge the ways I myself perpetuated a White theater program at the cost of others.

## All the World Is a Stage: Or Is It?

> Um, theater is so open, you can just be yourself. I think that within the walls of the theater there is something magical that happens that people can just be themselves. No matter where you are or what group you are from, you bind together for a good reason—which is the show. But that makes you come closer. (Gretchen, 17)

Indeed, in my teaching, I have found the theater to be a most liberating place. In a role we are allowed to be someone else for a while, even though we never fully escape who we are. It is a process that grants us permission to search and feel and connect to others in unique ways. Who we are, who we are perceived to be, what we are allowed to be are all parts of our lives, and this seems to become even more pronounced in the process of creating and becoming a character.

The masks we wear in our daily lives can be at times freeing while at other times suffocating. That is why in my first year at East it was refreshing to hear students talk about theater as "home" and as a space to "bring people together" and "be yourself." Indeed, in a large and sometimes intimidating high school, students need to find a place and feel a sense of belonging in school. All students need this. Which is why, after basking in the comments from my White students that theater was a place "that people come together," I was forced to realize that really only *some* people come together. Ultimately, in reflecting on these comments I came face to face with the painful reality that "coming together" had been appropriated by the White students and their White director.

To be sure, this wasn't a new reality for me, given my past experience at Central, but somehow at East I was temporarily lulled into complacency. Perhaps I had assumed the greater racial diversity at the school would naturally find its way to the stage. Indeed, it was the reiteration of the need for "color-blind casting" that supported not changing anything.

My White students promoted color blindness in multiple forms as the solution to our diversity "issues" in the theater program. In fact, when I later challenged this notion by staging *The Piano Lesson* again, many White students were quite threatened. I received an e-mail from one student that typified the threat that comes with challenging the status quo. The student wrote, "I've talked to numerous people (both Black and White, though that should hardly matter), and none of them have been amendable to the idea of playing up a particular race. No one wants to be reminded of differences beyond their control, and no one wants the drama department to be anything but enjoyable, inclusive, and good training for actors."

I remember being struck by the word *inclusive* when I read this e-mail. I also remember puzzling over the need to avoid difference at all cost. But in stepping back from this response and others like it, I can understand the ways that color blindness—or a professed belief in it—can aid in creating a community while not questioning the modes of maintenance of that community.

This complacency leads directly to a comforting belief in meritocracy— the idea that we all gain, we all lose, and we all have an equal chance to, in this case, participate in the theater community, take whatever classes we choose, or achieve or not achieve in high school. The sentiment among many of the White students I interviewed is summed up by this student's comment: "Eventually it will all work out—this cycle of losing and gaining. Everyone falls, everyone gains." If that were the case, then we need not push too hard or look at our own practices, which may be exclusionary.

## A Battle for Center Stage (New State, Similar Story)

My decision to produce *The Piano Lesson* this second time stemmed directly from my own commitment to de-center the Whiteness and the exclusionary practices I had replicated. Since moving to academia I have become acutely aware that we use terms like *de-center* without ever having the intention of seeing such a practice play out in real people's lives. I see my decision to direct *The Piano Lesson* again as a concrete example of attempting to de-center Whiteness. When I did the play at Central, it meant a great deal to me and to the students involved, but it was, to be honest, isolated. In developing as a teacher and through learning in the various multiracial settings, I had come to a much deeper understanding: that the experience of White people in this country does not need to be (nor should it be) the center of all, or the measurement of all, things good or worthy. To publicly announce my intention of casting, directing, and producing an all-Black play seemed a small step in taking the spotlight for a moment, so others could perhaps see themselves.

However, given the dominance of Whiteness in the program, the project did not go as smoothly as I would hope. Given that I needed to make sure that all students had an opportunity to participate, I needed to do another play. Each time I mounted a production of a play with an African American cast, I would simultaneously mount a production of a second play that allowed me to cast students from all backgrounds. At Central I had also directed *Under Milk Wood* by Dylan Thomas while *The Piano Lesson* was under production. At East, I selected *Prelude to a Kiss*.

What is interesting here to me, though, is that many of the White students expressed a sense of loss regarding my decision and complained of segregation. During auditions White students asked if they could audition for both shows. When I told them they could not, they were hurt and angry. It boggled my mind how threatened White students felt regarding this play. For the first time they were being denied something based on their race. To them this was unfair and, as one student put it, "damaging to humanity." The White students were not displaced. To lean on theater terms, I was asking them to *share the spotlight* for a bit.

Being a "good" White liberal, though, I must admit to being uncomfortable with the separatist nature of the two plays. It was important that we do both plays, and equally important that each cast feel a responsibility and connection to each other and to the other show. To that end I organized each rehearsal to begin with warm-ups together as a theater company. Additionally, I planned days within the rehearsal schedule during which students from both productions met the entire time together to discuss ideas, play games, eat, and generally attempt to gel as a community.

Despite these efforts, some of the White students resisted. From skipping theater community meetings to suggesting we create separate T-shirts for each show to complaining that *The Piano Lesson* kids were favored, these students made it clear that they were not part of the larger theater company and their loyalty remained with the other jilted members of *Prelude to a Kiss*.

As I write this I am reminded how frustrated and angry I was over the students' behavior. But I am now struck with how I still struggled to find the skills to meaningfully discuss interracial tensions without creating camps. My work at East cemented my role and desire to work as an ally in the struggle against racism. However, looking back at some of the memories of rage I felt at some of the White students, I realize how much I still needed to grow. Back then I still saw myself largely as the lone White hero seeking to do the right thing but lacking the tools to fully pull it off. Yet, even with this insight there is still the sting of resentment as I think back to the closing night of both shows.

For each closing-night ceremony we come together to say good-bye to the cast and crew and share final thoughts about the show. After these shows I talked a bit less and listened more. I heard some students claim how much they had learned and how grateful they were for the opportunity. But years later I still recall the negative. I heard White students claim they had put the show together themselves, even though they rehearsed with me four days a week. I heard them suggest that *The Piano Lesson* had struggled and that they were surprised and relieved that the cast had pulled it off.

I hear them. Then I force myself to stop and consider the moments that worked. For as much as this was a struggle, it was also a victory.

## Piano Lessons

At the first rehearsal for this second production of *The Piano Lesson*, something small but powerful occurred. As cast members came in and picked up their scripts and I began explaining the rehearsal and performance schedule, the front row of the auditorium began to fill with African American students. At the first few rehearsals it was just friends of cast members. After a week or two it was friends of friends, all interested in this play. The word had gotten out that the "drama lady" was doing a "Black" play and people wanted to see if this was real. One student stopped a teacher and asked, "Can they really do that?"

This was an important event, not just for the students in the play but also for their friends, for the community, and for the high school at large. As the weeks progressed, I was frequently stopped in the hallway by Black students who told me, "I want to be in a play." Later, at a basketball game, I was approached by a group of African American young women. One young woman whom I had never met asked, "Aren't you the one doing the Black play?" I told them I was, and they hugged me and thanked me. These experiences offer a glimmer of the collection of responses from African American students. They speak to me of a hunger to be recognized and to have their experiences counted and honored. In a school and society steeped in a color-blind ideal, these students relished the idea that another story could be told.

Just like when I was first teaching at Central, I had to position myself clearly in the role of learner. Although I had previous experience with this play and was seeking out and reading more playwrights of color, I entered with a willingness and need to listen and learn. Yes, I pushed and taught, but never did I suggest that my vision was complete or that my learning greater or more connected to the text. I do think this willingness came from working in such a diverse school and realizing the richness of the stories around me. I also think this willingness allowed us to grow close as a company. One night I started yelling that we were becoming a dysfunctional family, with everyone asking something of someone else. Cory, one of my actors, looked me in the eye and said, "That is what a good family is—you take care of each other."

The production was not flawless. The process was long and often tiring. The doubt that the students within the cast expressed about whether they could do it or not was, at times, paralyzing. But the sweetness in seeing the play come together and in watching the students create their characters, understand their roles, and own the stage was nothing short of magical. In the end we had relatively small audiences and poor press coverage. But for the school and the students involved in the production, that did not matter so much. I watched my students after opening night as they milled in the front of the stage smiling, laughing, and shaking hands with friends and family. They did not want to leave the moment even to take off their costumes.

Eventually the regular pace of school life reemerged, and with it came more lessons about the larger issues of inequity *we were all facing*. Soon after the play I learned that one of the lead actors was being referred to special education by his English teacher. This young man learned huge amounts of dialogue, came to understand his character deeply, and led the cast to understand nuances of a very complex text. I recall seeing a worksheet he was supposed to complete containing a page of sentences with certain words blanked out, and he was to fill in the correct word. This was English? This young man had shown an advanced understanding of text and subtext along with a remarkable ability to interpret and act, and yet these skills were unmarked and unrewarded. For him, taking that costume off meant facing a school that saw him not as a remarkable actor and performer but as an indifferent student incapable of complex work. I gradually realized that the work of being an anti-racist educator was much larger than I had ever imagined.

The reality is that anti-racist work will never be as tidy as a curtain call following a triumphant production. Yet, it is in that small world of theater within high school that worlds opened up for me, and many of my own shortcomings and biases were forced to the fore.

In the year 2013 some may argue we have achieved a healthier picture. My lessons from working in schools and from my students who were my teachers tell me that there are many students not portrayed on our stages, much less honored in our classrooms. I close with words from my director's notes from the *Piano Lesson/Prelude* project. I think they show my growth as an educator through the work we had to do then and still need to do now.

> These pieces are presented in the continued hope that we can work toward providing places on our stages, in our schools, and within our lives for multiple voices to be heard . . . we must challenge ourselves to define diversity in a way that does not push all difference aside in the name of unity. We need to continue to work to transform our stages, schools, and communities so that we expect and truly celebrate the multiple diversities each contain. The plays are a piece of that project.

## Journal Questions

1. Tara grew up hearing from her parents, "We don't treat people that way." In your journal write the line "We don't treat people that way" five

times, and then let your writing go and see where it takes you. Don't edit your responses; just go with the line and see where you land.

2. In your journal write what you would say to Michael after he said to you, "You may be a nice lady. You may even talk about justice, but I will never trust you because you are White."

3. Write a letter to Tara in your journal in response to her comment, "Look at me doing these good things for these students, especially all these poor, Black young women, I am good." Tell her why her intent was good but misguided.

4. In your journal defend or disagree with Tara's decision to allow her students to use the word "nigger" in their production of August Wilson's play *The Piano Lesson*. Does it make a difference that the play was presented to an "almost all-White audience"?

5. Tara writes that she is still struggling "to find the skills to meaningfully discuss interracial tensions [in school] without creating camps." In your journal write how you have solved this problem or about your struggle with it.

*Kat Richter in 2011*
*(Photo credit: Brian Mengini)*

# 9

# TAP DANCING
# ON TILE

Sidestepping Failure at Guilford
Elementary School

*Kat Richter*

"I assumed that they would connect with the photographs of Savion Glover, Gregory Hines, the Nicholas Brothers, and Bill 'Bojangles' Robinson simply because they shared a skin color in common."

I wore the biggest hoop earrings I owned on my first day at Guilford Elementary School. It begged to reason, or so I thought at the time, that my mother's Puerto Rican heritage was more "ethnic" than my dad's northern European ancestry, and if I wanted to relate to the all-Black student body at Guilford Elementary, I would need to look as "ethnic" as possible. As such, I dug through my jewelry box for the hoop earrings, outlined my lips in a dark liner and spent nearly an hour combing my curly hair into submission, resulting in a slick, straight pony tail.

Slinging my lesson plans into my bag, I felt confident that I looked the part: urban, cool, and of course, Puerto Rican. Not once, as I headed to the parking lot and carefully arranged my Baltimore map on the passenger's seat of my car, did it occur to me that I was a walking pastiche of a modern-day Latina, better suited for a late-night comedy sketch than an inner-city elementary school.

Forgive my naïveté. I was 21 years old and just starting my senior year at Goucher College. I had been programmed with the desire to "make a difference" in the world, to "be the change" I wanted to see and to "think globally but act locally." Guilford Elementary seemed like the perfect place to alleviate my White guilt, and although I had no formal training in education, the volunteer coordinator at the Johns Hopkins Center for Social Concern did not seem to mind.

"When would you like to start?" she had asked, flipping through my application.

"Next week?" I asked hopefully.

"Fine, fine. What would you like to teach?"

"Tap," I replied. "I'm a dance major."

"Excellent," she nodded. "I'm sure the kids in the after-school program will like that. Would you like me to assign another volunteer to work with you?"

"No thanks," I replied, tucking the volunteer handbook into my bag. "I'll be fine on my own."

I was, admittedly, a bit nervous about finding the school—Guilford Elementary was a far cry from the bucolic college campus where I lived in an all-girls dorm—and I was anxious about how the students would perceive me, but as I left campus, I knew one thing for sure: I was a good teacher, and not only that, I was a good *dance* teacher. I had seen, first hand, how dance could inspire a student, even when they thought they had failed at everything else. I had seen adolescents from broken homes transcend the difficulties of their personal lives upon entering the studio. I had witnessed friendships forged, transformations made, and insecurities forgotten, and I was sure that my contribution to Guilford's after-school program would come as a welcome relief to the daily routine of homework help and in-school suspension.

As I pulled into the parking lot, I could already picture the choreography, the costumes, and the pep talk I would give the kids backstage, and once the news of our success reached the superintendent, she would recognize the value of arts education. In the coming months, test scores would skyrocket. Funding for the arts would come pouring in. Registration for my tap class would shoot through the roof, and as for my students, they would eventually receive full scholarships to well-endowed private liberal arts colleges, from which they would graduate with majors in education, sports science, and dance, naturally.

That is how I had it all planned out in my head. Reality, of course, was an entirely different matter.

"Hi," I announced, weaving my way through a siege of spitballs toward a seemingly "responsible adult" in the corner of the cafeteria. "I'm Kat Richter."

"Who?" the woman yelled over the noise. Then, before I could answer, she turned and shouted across the room, "Nehemiah! Don't make me come over there!"

"I'm one of the volunteers from the Johns Hopkins Center for Social Concern," I prompted.

"Right," she said finally. "I'm Linda. Ballet?"

"Tap," I corrected.

"Oh, you're the one who emailed me," she said. "You'll have to do without the wooden floors you asked for."

"That's okay," I assured her. I knew better than to expect a proper dance studio in a public school, but I figured there was no harm in asking.

"The older students are in the gym watching the basketball game," she continued, "but once they come back you can teach your class over in that corner."

Glancing around the room, as the students continued tossing cartons of milk across the lunch tables and launching spitballs into the air, I started to get nervous. There was no way I could teach a dance class in a *corner* of the cafeteria.

"I don't mean to be difficult," I implored, "but isn't there a classroom we can go to? Somewhere a bit quieter maybe?"

"Quieter?" she laughed. "Honey, when you find someplace quieter, be sure to let me know." As an afterthought, she added, "I'll see if any of the classrooms are still unlocked. But don't get your hopes up." With that, she disappeared, leaving me the only White person in the room, alone in the cafeteria. I smiled shyly at a couple of the students and they smiled shyly back, but as the minutes passed I started to think I had made a big mistake.

Finally Linda returned with a line of students trailing behind her. "The basketball game is over and Room 49 is unlocked," she announced. "They're all yours."

"What we gonna do?" one student demanded.

"You a *real* ballerina?" asked another.

"They got any more candy in the cafeteria?"

Before I could formulate a response, the students erupted into a chorus of complaints.

"Man, why we gotta dance?"

"I ain't dancin', dancin's for girls!"

"Shut up, De'ron, you *is* a girl!" (To which De'ron replied, "Oh yeah? Why don't you come over here and make me shut up?")

Individually, I could have answered their questions. But of course, there was no time for that.

"Enough!" shouted Linda. "You all better listen to Miss Kat, and if she gives me a bad report, you can forget about dance lessons next week. Are we clear?"

"Yeah," a few of the students replied, shuffling into a straight line against the wall.

Turning to De'ron, Linda shouted, "Are we *clear*, De'ron?"

"Whatever," he mumbled, scuffing his feet on the tile floor.

"Excuse me?" she demanded.

De'ron remained silent.

"De'ron," she intoned, "I'm not gonna ask you again." Some of the other students began to giggle. Unsure as to whether I should be more offended by De'ron's disrespectful behavior or by Linda's browbeating approach to education, I found an excuse to fiddle with my CD player.

"Fine!" De'ron finally shouted. "We're clear."

"Good," she replied. "Off you go."

I did my best to look authoritative as I led the students to Room 49. Unfortunately, the success of my authoritative look was compromised by the fact that I had neglected to ask Linda where to find Room 49. Turning to a short girl with long braids—she looked harmless enough—I said, in my best "responsible adult" voice, "Remind me. Is Room 49 on this floor or upstairs?"

"Upstairs," she replied. "Is your name really 'Miss Cat?'"

"Yes," I answered with a smile.

"I'm Mercedes," she announced.

Before I could say, "nice to meet you," two girls elbowed their way to the front of the line.

"I'm Nashawn" the first said.

"And I'm Nashawna" the second declared.

Identical twins named Nashawn and Nashawna? I waited for the telltale giggles of a joke at the new teacher's expense but there were none—those were their real names.

Marching up the stairs with my new best friends Mercedes, Nashawn, and Nashawna fighting to stand next to me, I thought, *Well now,* this *is more like it.* De'ron might be a lost cause but at least the girls would appreciate my efforts.

In that moment, with that glimmer of hope, I let my guard down. The boys raced up the stairs ahead of me, De'ron and Nehemiah in the lead.

"Wait!" I commanded. I might not know much about teaching in the public school system, but I knew that a group of children running down the halls after hours without a teacher was a definite no-no. Of course, the boys didn't listen. And when I tried to harness their energy by giving them a constructive task ("Can you please push the desks to the side of the classroom so we have space to dance?"), they flung the desks into the wall, trying to crush their classmates in the process.

When I asked the students to form two lines, they refused. And when I blasted my CD of Duke Ellington jazz standards in the hopes of establishing some sort of basic aesthetic connection (Ellington was Black, after all), they started fighting.

"Hey!" I shouted. I had never shouted at my students, not once in my entire career as a dance teacher. I respected my students, and for the most part, they respected me. But respect, in this case, was definitely not working.

"Hey!" I shouted again, louder this time. De'ron was wrestling with Nehemiah, who had, as far as I could tell, disrespected De'ron's momma. "De'ron!" I demanded. "Cut it out!" It had all happened so fast—one minute I was begging the students to give Ellington a chance, and the next I was having flashbacks to a fight that had broken out in the cafeteria when I was in fifth grade. In that particular instance, the gym teacher had jumped in to break it up; the result for her was a concussion and the end of her teaching career.

I could jump in, but what would happen to the other kids if I earned myself a concussion in the process? "Fight, fight, fight!" they began to chant. My mind raced as I tried to figure out what to do. The nearest adults were downstairs at the other end of the school, well beyond shouting range; if I tried to break up the fight and *failed* there was no telling what sort of *Lord of the Flies* scenario might ensue. I had to take charge.

"Everybody listen up!" I bellowed, climbing atop the teacher's desk to make myself heard. Then, possessed by some unknown force, I shouted, "Nehemiah, say you're sorry! De'ron, cut it out! The rest of you shut your mouths and sit down. Are we clear?"

I like to think my imposing presence had the intended effect, but really it was Linda and a handful of adult volunteers who suddenly barged into the classroom that saved the day.

"What's going on in here?" Linda demanded. The room fell silent. "You ought to be ashamed of yourselves," she admonished, looking from one student to the next. "Is this how we treat guests in our school?"

"No," they mumbled in unison.

"I said, *Is this how we treat guests in our school?*"

"No!" they shouted.

"I didn't think so," she surmised. "Now, everybody line up. And De'ron, you say you're sorry to Miss Kat."

"Sorry," he mumbled, staring at the floor.

"Sorry what?" she demanded.

"Sorry, Miss Kat."

"And as for the rest of you," she continued, turning back to the group of students leaning against the wall. "I had better have a good report from Miss Kat next week, *if* she even comes back after today. Are we clear?"

"Yes," they chanted.

"Good. Now, everyone, back downstairs."

For a while I just stood there, too stunned to follow. I pretended that I needed to put my CDs back into the right cases, that I needed to unlace my tap shoes, that I needed to check off all that we had "accomplished" on my lesson plans, but I just sank down into a child-size chair, feeling about as small as the occupant it was designed to hold.

I was naïve, yes, and inexperienced, and feeling rather unequal to the task of teaching 30 inner-city students to tap dance, but I knew one thing for sure. I couldn't let them think they had beaten me. I'm not sure how I knew this—certainly not through any personal experience with physical violence and codes of honor—but I had to walk back through the cafeteria on my way out. I had to look De'ron in the eye and let him know I would be back next week. I had to stand tall, and I had to hold back the tears—which I knew would be coming—until I got back to campus.

But it wasn't De'ron I encountered on my way out, nor was it Nehemiah. It was Mercedes. She came running over to me and demanded, "Miss Kat, you comin' back next week?"

"Yes," I assured her, forcing a smile, "I'll see you on Tuesday, okay?"

"Okay," she answered. Satisfied with my response, she ran back to Nashawn and Nashawna, presumably to share the good news. Without bothering to wait for their reaction, I headed straight to my car, flipped open my cell phone and dialed my mom.

"Mom? It's me." I sobbed, "I'm the worst teacher in the whole entire world. . . ."

Week two, she assured me, would be better. It had to be better, I agreed. It certainly couldn't be *worse*. After my mom's pep talk, a quick makeover in the Student Center bathroom, and a huge serving of dining hall ice cream,

I returned to my dorm with a renewed sense of enthusiasm. Rome wasn't built in a day, I reminded myself, tossing my old lesson plans into the trash. Of course my second week would be better.

It wasn't.

I kept the students distracted enough to avoid another fight, but once again, Linda had to "rescue" me 20 minutes into the lesson. They hated my Duke Ellington CDs. They couldn't care less about the famous African American tap dancers whose pictures I had printed at the computer lab, despite my attempts to convince them that tap was a part of *their* heritage. Furthermore, as I begged the students to *brush*, rather than stomp, their feet against the floor, I began to doubt that any of them would emerge from Miss Kat's Tuesday Tap Class having mastered even the basics of tap, let alone an actual, award-winning routine.

De'ron spoke for the entire class when he complained, "Miss, why we gotta do tap? Can't we go outside and play basketball?"

In hindsight, I should have known that there was no reason for a bunch of inner-city kids from Baltimore to like Ellington—why would they? I assumed that they would connect with the photographs of Savion Glover, Gregory Hines, the Nicholas Brothers, and Bill "Bojangles" Robinson simply because they shared a skin color in common. And I thought they would recognize the value of an arts education—a *free* arts education—and so I took it personally when De'ron announced he would rather go play basketball.

I got back in my car, called my mom, and broke down into tears again.

By week three, this was becoming a bit of a routine. By week four, having yelled myself hoarse, I realized something had to change. Sitting on the floor of my dorm, surrounded by yet another set of abandoned lesson plans and my "Superstars of Tap" photographs, I tried to figure out what *exactly* was going wrong.

First was the size of the class: 30 students ranging from first to fifth grade. It wasn't so much the number of students that was the problem but rather the range in ages, learning styles, and attention spans. Wanting to "reach" as many students as possible, I had assured Linda I could handle as many students as wanted to tap, but clearly I could not.

Another problem was discipline. The students refused to wait turns when practicing steps across the floor, and I could not, for the life of me, get them to stand in a line.

They hated my music. They would rather be playing basketball. They didn't care about artistic expression or dance history or playing music with their feet. In short, my tap class was just an excuse to get out of the crowded cafeteria for an hour on Tuesday afternoons.

There were some things I couldn't change, such as the fact that we were tap dancing, slipping and sliding, on a tile floor. I couldn't change the fact that the students didn't share my passion for tap. I couldn't change the fact that my roster fluctuated from one week to the next, making it impossible to progress beyond the basics. But I could change the few things within my control: I could change the age range, my music, and my overall approach to arts education. I still believed that it was important for the kids to learn tap history right alongside the actual steps, but I realized that the class was not about what *I* wanted to teach the kids; it was about what *they* wanted to learn. If I wanted to impart a bit of cultural knowledge on the side, I would have to do it on their terms.

"Listen up," I commanded the next week as the students weaved tentatively through the photographs I had mounted, laminated, and taped to the floor. "We're gonna have a proper dance class today, in a straight line, so everyone find a picture and stand on it." My "Superstars" collection had expanded to include Eleanor Powell, Ginger Rogers, Gene Kelly, and stars of every color and age. Thanks to a roll of contact paper purchased at a nearby office supply store, they were now indestructible.

The class was smaller this week: just third through fifth graders. It broke my heart to turn away the younger students, but I promised I would find them another teacher; until then they could take ballet from another of the Hopkins volunteers. Instructing De'ron to stand on Savion Glover's photograph, I sent Nehemiah to stand on Gregory Hines far on the other side of the classroom *before* they could start fighting.

I held my breath as I popped a new CD into the boom box. I had splurged on Blow Pops and—my *pièce de résistance*—Usher's latest album.

"Here we go," I smiled—I just *knew* they were going to love Usher— "Five, six, seven, eight!" But Mercedes had other ideas. "Miss!" she shouted, crossing her arms. "This is old-school!"

"We want Chris Brown," Nashawn shouted.

"Chris Brown!" Nashawna echoed. So much for my knowledge of cutting-edge hip-hop music. To squelch the impending mutiny, I promised Chris Brown for the following week and *extra* lollipops for good behavior in the meantime. After class, instead of crying, I drove straight to the mall, where I forked over the remainder of my paycheck for the self-titled debut album of Chris Brown.

By the time Christmas break rolled around, things were looking up. I had recruited another volunteer from Goucher to teach the younger students, and my class, which now averaged about 15 students each week, had finally mastered the art of tap's most basic step, the shuffle. Most exciting of all, the Johns Hopkins Community Center had agreed to finance the purchasing of tap shoes for the entire class, and at the prospect of owning *real* tap shoes, the students were almost—dare I say it?—enthusiastic about Tuesday afternoons with Miss Kat.

It was, therefore, with great shock that I returned to Guilford in January to find nearly a third of my students gone. "De'ron got expelled," explained Mercedes.

"And what about Nehemiah?" I asked. Despite a rough start, Nehemiah was turning into one of the best dancers in the class. Mercedes just shrugged. Evidently, Nehemiah was in foster care; his disappearances were a regular occurrence.

"Sometimes he sleeps at the school," Mercedes informed me. "He'll probably be back. You got our tap shoes yet?"

I nodded, and managed to get through the rest of the lesson, the trying on of the shoes, and the arguing over sizes and styles, but when I got back to campus the tears returned. De'ron and Nehemiah were just 10 years old. What could a 10-year-old *possibly* have done that was so bad as to earn him an expulsion? More important, how was anyone who has been expelled at the age of 10 by the very system that promised "No Child Left Behind" supposed to amount to anything in life?

Nehemiah returned, just as Mercedes predicted he would, but I never saw De'ron again.

By springtime, I was feeling confident enough to interject a smattering of Ellington into the weekly tributes to Chris Brown. I brought in my laptop and invited the students to crowd around for a clip from Nick Castle's 1989 film *Tap*. As long as we were watching videos, they didn't object to my tap history lessons.

I was falling in love with my students: Mercedes, who ran up to me in the cafeteria on my arrival, demanding, "Look Miss! Look, I practiced!"; Nashawn and Nashawna, who were always so smiley that I still couldn't tell them apart; little Emmet, who didn't care that a pair of girl's patent leather Mary Janes were the only tap shoes I could find to fit him; Kamau, a recent transplant from Georgia whose perfect, polite Southern drawl was slowly giving way to the urban Baltimore vernacular of his classmates; and finally Nehemiah, who, despite the many traumas of his home life, had occasional moments of brilliance that inspired me to keep coming back to Guilford week after week.

I had accepted the fact that a full-scale year-end recital was out of the question, but driving back to campus one night, I had an idea.

"We're going on a field trip," I announced the following Tuesday. Goucher's annual dance concert was coming up, and somehow I managed to navigate the bureaucracy of both Goucher's dance department and Guilford's administrative offices to score a dozen free tickets, a van, and Linda as a chaperone.

"Where to?" Nehemiah demanded.

"A dance concert," I replied, hauling a portable TV onto the desk.

"Are there gonna be real ballerinas there?" Nashawn and Nashawna asked in unison.

"Yes." Goucher regularly hosted guest choreographers of world renown—the program boasted both a Balanchine piece and Nijinsky's avant-garde *Afternoon of the Faun* that year—and the dance department was top-notch.

"There will be ballet dancers, and modern dancers, *and* tap dancers," I explained, trying to hide my personal sense of triumph at having finally witnessed tap's long-awaited recognition at Goucher. "Now," I instructed, loading an Alvin Ailey film into the VCR as an introduction to a crash course in dance appreciation, "watch this."

I knew better than to expect a mature reaction to men in tights, so I figured I had better give the students a chance to get the giggles out of their systems.

"Miss," Nehemiah announced, right on cue, "that's gay."

Already a step ahead of him, I traded Ailey for Mikhail Baryshnikov. "This is one of the most famous dancers of all time," I informed the students. "And he wasn't gay. In fact, he had lots and lots of girlfriends. Check out his jumps!"

Nehemiah looked unconvinced.

"Come on," I urged, pointing to a particularly masculine lift. "You don't have to *like* ballet, but just look at his muscles. He was just as strong as an athlete."

Unimpressed, Nehemiah shook his head.

"I bet you can't carry a girl across the stage like that!" I finally challenged. *That* would show him—at least, it would have shown Emmet or Kamau, but not Nehemiah. Without missing a beat, he grabbed Mercedes around the waist and carried her across the room.

"Okay, okay," I conceded, trying not to laugh as Mercedes kicked him in the shins. "Maybe you can."

Ending the lesson with a quick lecture on audience etiquette, I assured the students I would come and say "hi" to them after the show.

On the way back to campus, I stopped at the grocery store to pick up some chocolate (I needed provisions to finish my term papers). Strolling absentmindedly down the aisles, I ran into a fellow dance major from Goucher. She was doing a minor in education and as such had been recently placed with one of the Baltimore County schools.

"How's it going over at Guilford?" she asked.

"Not bad," I replied, "considering the circumstances. It's a pretty rough neighborhood. I think three quarters of the students qualify for free or reduced-price lunch."

"Ninety percent of my students qualify," she announced proudly.

"Well maybe it's actually closer to 90 percent at Guilford," I replied.

It wasn't until she disappeared around the corner that the real gravity of the situation hit me: whether 75 or 90 percent of my Guilford students qualified for free or reduced-price lunch didn't matter, because either way at least *some* of the students coming to the concert would depend on a meal from the cafeteria. By inviting them to the matinee performance, I would be depriving them of their lunch.

The morning of the show, I puttered around backstage with more than the usual amount of stage fright. Not only was this the first time that my peers and professors would see me tap, but I had *students* in the audience, at least I would, as soon as Linda found the theater.

Finally, as I tightened the screws on my taps for the third time, my cell phone rang. "We're here!" Linda announced.

I ran through the dressing rooms, nearly crashing into a classmate who was dressed as Nijinsky's faun in a spotted leotard.

"Where's the fire, Kat?" he yelled as I bounded up the steps to the lobby.

"My kids are here!" I shouted back. "I have to give them their lunches!"

Distributing the brightly colored bags of juice boxes, bananas, and muffins, I knelt down next to the students for one final warning. "Remember what we talked about," I instructed. "You don't have to *like* the dances—"

"But you have to respect the dancers," Kamau finished for me.

"Right! Okay. See you after the show!"

Closing my eyes as I took my place in the wings, I folded my hands and made my usual preperformance plea: *Please God, don't let me fuck up.* The words of my mentor, Deborah Mitchell, founder and artistic director of the New Jersey Tap Ensemble, came flooding back to me: "Don't hold anything back," she used to say backstage. "You've got to dance like this might be your last performance." And she was right. Although I hoped it wouldn't be my last performance, I knew it might very well be the last time that my students would go to the theater.

"Take the 'A' Train" filled the auditorium. I stepped into the spotlight and I danced—for my professors, the majority of whom still dismissed tap as "recreational" dance form; for my peers, who weren't much better; for the "Superstars of Tap," in all their laminated glory; and for my students, who watched silently and cheered at all the right moments—as though I might never dance again.

After the show, Mercedes confessed, "Miss, when that boy came out dressed like that deer I wanted to laugh but I covered my mouth."

"That's fine," I assured her. Then, before I could stop myself, I asked, "Did anyone recognize the music from the tap piece?"

Nashawn and Nashawna shrugged. Emmet scratched his head, and Nehemiah stared at the floor. Finally, Kamau piped up. "It sounded familiar."

Familiar? That was good enough for me.

After the concert, I informed the students that we would be having a small recital and a party to celebrate their accomplishments. "Everyone's invited," I announced, distributing the flyers I had printed out for their parents and teachers. Ever the optimist, I had great hopes for the recital. The students would perform two numbers: first a chair dance to Chris Brown and then a traditional tap routine, the Shim Sham Shimmy, to "Sunny Side of the Street." In addition, each would read a short passage about their favorite "Superstar of Tap" to demonstrate the academic ramifications of arts education. I borrowed my brother's video camera, and he agreed to produce a professional-grade DVD of the performance, which I could then mail to each student. I fired off an email to a children's publishing company, asking if they would donate copies of Savion Glover's *My Life in Tap* for me to give to the students, and I baked two dozen tap-shaped cookies for the big day.

Two dozen cookies were about two dozen too many. I arrived at two thirty to decorate the classroom, but by three o'clock, only Mercedes, Emmet, Kamau, and Nashawn had shown up.

"Are any of your parents coming?" I asked, trying to hide my disappointment.

The students shrugged.

"Aunts and uncles?" I asked hopefully. "Brothers and sisters?"

Just then, Nehemiah tumbled past the classroom with two women in his wake. I breathed a sigh of relief—we would have an audience after all! But the women weren't there for the show, and Nehemiah was crying.

"What's wrong?" I asked, stepping out into the hall. I had never seen Nehemiah cry before, but he just sniffled and stared at the floor.

"His behavior is totally inappropriate," I overheard one woman say to the other.

"Totally inappropriate," she agreed. They kept right on discussing Nehemiah as if he wasn't even there.

"What's going on?" I asked the women, wondering who they were. Nehemiah's family? Teachers? Social workers?

"Nehemiah's in trouble," one replied.

"Again," the other added. Nehemiah just kept crying, staring at the floor and shaking.

"Can he stay for the show?" I requested. "The tap class is having a performance."

"No." The women replied in unison, grabbing Nehemiah by the forearms.

"Wait!" I pleaded. "Let me at least get him his tap shoes." I ran back into the classroom and grabbed Nehemiah's shoes, the Certificate of Achievement printed with his name, and two tap-shaped cookies. I gave Nehemiah a hug and handed him his shoes in silence because I knew I too would start crying if I tried to say anything.

Feeling completely dejected, I turned back to the classroom. I couldn't "save" Nehemiah, but as the old saying goes, the show must go on.

"Wait!" a voice called down the hall. "I'm here!" It was Nashawna.

She ran down the corridor, followed by an elderly man. "Nashawna was home sick today," he explained, "but she said she just *had* to be here."

In the end, the only audience member was Guilford's vice principal, and in hindsight, I suspect she didn't even come to see the kids; she came for me, the poor White girl trying to change the world with a dozen pairs of tap shoes and two dozen tap-shaped cookies.

My year at Guilford did *not* inspire me to become a teacher. Guilford left me hating the public school system, the foster care system, and all the other systems that had, as far as I was concerned, failed Nehemiah.

I have no idea what has become of any of the students, and I probably never will. I graduated from Goucher in May 2007, and aside from one last trip to Guilford Elementary School to throw an end-of-the-year party for the kids, I have never returned.

If I go back, I'll find out what's become of Nehemiah, and I'd rather hope for the impossible than learn the truth. If I go back, I might find out that the year I spent at Guilford didn't make an ounce of difference in their lives, and I'm not ready to accept that.

After graduation I took a job in development at a nonprofit theater in Philadelphia, where I wrote grants for arts education programs; fund-raising, I found, was less heartbreaking than teaching. A year later I moved to London to complete my master's in dance anthropology. I learned that musical taste is something that must be developed. I learned that it's racist to insist that Black people are born with a sense of rhythm, and I discovered that I have a knack for academic research. I graduated with distinction, and my professors' encouragement to go on for my doctorate. On returning to the United States I was invited to give my first lecture.

It is 2010, four years after I taught my first class at Guilford Elementary School. I am standing before a class of 30 community college students, and their professor has told me not to take it personally if they get up and leave during the middle of my lecture. They do it all the time, she assures me, and "Dance Under the Reign of Henry VIII" is not a particularly "sexy" subject. Despite my preparation, I'm nervous. These students are adults. My mind flashes back to the moment I climbed on top of a desk at Guilford, screaming, "Are we clear?" and I wish I had never agreed to give this lecture in the first place.

But then I think of Nehemiah. I think he could be one of those boys leaning against the wall someday, and I pray, *Please God, don't let me fuck up.* And I don't, because I know better now; I've left my hoop earrings at home, and I know, thanks to my students at Guilford Elementary School, that this is where I belong. Here, before a group of 30 inner-city kids, is where dance and hope intersect.

## Journal Questions

1. Kat's passion was dance. In your journal, flow write about your passions in life. Can they be actualized in teaching?

2. Down a rough road, Kat came to see what she couldn't change and what she could change. Journal about an experience you had that brought you to that kind of knowing.

3. Journal about what your expectations are for teaching children of color. List both the ideal and the realistic.

# 10

# A QUESTION
# OF BALANCE

My Journey of Cultural Evolution

*Tabitha Dell'Angelo*

*Tabitha Dell'Angelo at graduate school*

"Once I asked my grandmother what she thought about my going to the prom with one of my Black friends and she said she would disown me. I asked her, 'Really, you're kidding. You would really never talk to me again?' And she said, 'Yes, I would miss you, but I would disown you.'"

## My First Memories of Culture

Growing up in South Philadelphia in the 1970s I could have easily believed that the entire world was Italian, except that I often heard my grandmother complain that "the Chinese were moving in." Although, I was aware that "the Irish live on 2nd Street" and "the Blacks live in North Philly," in my little world of South Philadelphia I was surrounded by Italy—American style. My family primarily spoke English, but the older generations frequently threw Italian around, especially when I wasn't supposed to know what they were talking about.

My grandparents' house was my favorite place to go. It was a brownstone row house just like all the others, but when you walked inside, it was a different world. The first thing that greeted you was an orange tree that sat next to the staircase, and in the backyard was a garden with lots of vegetables and three fig trees. This might not seem like a big deal—to have a garden in your backyard—but in Philadelphia backyards were 9-by-14 slabs of concrete. However, my grandfather's backyard had a middle path with things growing on both sides and overhead. Inside the house, you would often find strings full of peppers hanging throughout to dry.

The upstairs in this house was another adventure. I wasn't allowed upstairs, but I took a chance whenever I could. I would dash directly to my grandmother's dresser. On her dresser was a huge jewelry box with angels and Jesus on it, with a little door in front and another door in back. And if I could get the doors open before my mother called to me, I would find one stick of gum that I always took.

My family lived all around me. When I walked to school I would pass my Aunt Rosie, Aunt Pudgie, and Aunt Midge's house. If I cut through an alley instead of staying on the main street my mother would know because one of the aunts would call to say I didn't pass the house. Often, I would see one of my uncles on the way—Squinteye, Ray Ray, Diddy, Georgie—or one of my grandfather's friends. Even if they weren't related they still considered themselves family.

I had limited interactions with children or adults who did not look like me until second grade. That year a girl with beautiful brown skin showed up in my classroom. I didn't understand the controversy over her presence. In Catholic school we learned that all people were brothers and sisters in the eyes of God. When I saw a stranger on the street or someone peeing against a wall I thought about this. If I thought something negative about someone, like the people who made fun of the Vietnamese vendors on 9th street because of their accents, I reminded myself that God loved them too.

I could not understand why others made disparaging remarks about another person based on skin color or ethnicity; didn't everyone know we were all brothers and sisters? So when this little brown-skinned girl showed up in my classroom I was mesmerized. I couldn't believe she was real and there, in my class. I imagined or assumed that children who didn't look like or sound like me and the other kids at my school went to school somewhere else. I didn't know where, but I expected to see them out shopping with my mom or maybe on TV, but not in my class. Having this exotic creature with her beautiful name, Puja, within an arm's reach left me curious and desperately wanting to be her friend.

The teacher sat her right in front in the middle row. I sat halfway down the row next to hers. With her back to me I couldn't get her attention. I wanted to be her friend, but I didn't know how to make that happen.

At that time my mother, my brother, and I lived with my grandparents and my two uncles. We moved in with them because my parents couldn't make it on their own and my father had left for Texas. My mom and grandmother both said that he was looking for work. I missed my father's smiles and hugs.

In my grandparents' home everyone seemed stressed out all the time. My grandmother yelled a lot and my mother never seemed happy. On the other hand, my grandfather owned the local butcher shop and we had plenty of food. The house had the warm smell of meat cooking and the lettuce and tomato salad my grandmother made, drenched in olive oil and vinegar and doused with tons of salt.

Living with my grandparents caused other anxieties. This house wasn't a safe place to be. One of my uncles was drug addicted and often stole from the family. The other uncle was a paranoid schizophrenic, and as a child, I perceived the symptoms of his illness as disdain for me. He never looked at me or spoke to me; he talked about me instead of to me. For instance, "Ma, tell Tabitha to sit on the other couch so I can sit down" and "Make her move her head so I can see the TV" were common requests. He wasn't abusive, but he seemed annoyed by my presence. Because he didn't look at me I knew he disliked me intensely.

As a child, I suffered with asthma and allergies, yet the five adults I lived with smoked in the house. The doctor's suggestions included, "No smoking near Tabitha, no cats, and get rid of stuffed animals because they harbor dust." In response, all of my stuffed animals were thrown away—the cats and cigarettes stayed. Everyone in the house was dealing with their own stress and had no compassion for a little girl who threatened their pleasure of smoking. One day while watching my mom brush her hair in the bathroom mirror I began coughing. She hit me with the brush and yelled, "Stop faking it, you're faking it." I tried to stop coughing but began crying and gasping for breath, only making the coughing worse.

Back at school my teacher announced that the little brown-skinned girl, Puja, was ill and wouldn't be back at school for a while. I volunteered to take her work to her house so she could keep up with the class. I suspected that my mother would be okay with this, because when I told my family about Puja, her name seemed to signal to my mother that she was of Indian descent. However, a comment was made that she would probably smell like curry, because "they all do."

Overwhelmed by a sense of adventure, I prepared to deliver Puja's homework. Where did she live? What was her house like? What was curry, and how did it smell? When I came home with the note from the teacher explaining I volunteered to deliver Puja's homework, my mother just rolled her eyes and laughed, "Why did you do this? I don't have time for this. We don't know these people." I remember that she spoke to my grandmother (Nani) about it, and they agreed that I was doing a nice thing and they wouldn't be angry with me. Mom's plan was to walk to Puja's house with me, make a quick drop off, and return home.

We walked to Puja's house at night, and my mother seemed nervous. Puja lived on a street where every house had a big porch, the sidewalks were wide enough for two people to walk side by side, and there were trees planted all along the way. We rang her doorbell. I loved when a house had a doorbell; it seemed fancy. I also imagined she had blue toilet water, which to me was also a sign of great class and wealth. As we stood at her door I worried that my mother would be abrupt or rude to Puja or her family. Then a young couple answered the door. The mom had the same brown complexion as Puja, and the dad was a bit darker. The family smiled at us, and I looked up at my mother's face and saw she was smiling back at them.

They invited us in and I didn't know what to do. On the way over my mother expressly stated that if they invited us in we should decline and that I should not make a fuss about it. But I think the warm smiles and the absence of curry smell confused my mother enough that we both crossed the threshold into the living room. We didn't go very far. Puja's mother offered us tea, but we just stood near the doorway while the moms chatted about school and Puja's being ill. I handed over a huge stack of books and papers. Puja and I sat down in front of their couch and stared at one another and smiled but didn't really speak. Sitting in Puja's living room was calming and comfortable. Her home was warm and quiet; I could have laid down and fallen asleep.

On our way home my mother held my hand and said, "They were really nice people. It was kind of you to help Puja with her work." The next morning she told me I could drop off Puja's work by myself the following day. That was the last time I delivered Puja's work, because after that she was feeling better. The family gave me a silver cross as a thank-you gift. I walked home proudly with the box, excited about showing it to my mother. My family fussed over the gift for quite a while, and we hung the cross in my bedroom. I still have the cross packed away somewhere, and every time I come across it I am reminded of Puja and her family and how they challenged my family to open their hearts.

## Family Stories

### *Toddlerhood*

After my interaction with the Indian girl at school my family began telling stories about how I would always talk to anyone. They told me a story (that they still tell) about when I was a baby. My mother was at the welfare office and waiting in line. There was a Black man in front of her.

"You kept reaching out for him. Finally, he turned around and said he would hold you. I told him, 'no,' and he said, 'I'm not going to hurt her, and she clearly wants to come with me.'" Finally, my mother let him hold me, and I seemed content. My mother says that she was very nervous about this and kept her eye on him. When I hear this I have conflicting feelings about it. First, it is nice to know that she felt protective of me. On the other hand, what did she think he was going to do—grab me and run away?

Every time I think about this story I wonder what this means, for a baby to be so content sitting with and being held by a stranger. Over the years, when the story was told, I wore it like a badge of honor, proof that I was inherently not racist.

### *Elementary and Middle School*

When I was in elementary school we moved from Philadelphia to New Jersey. At my new school I had Black students in my class. This was new to me, and at first I didn't exactly know what to make of it. I assumed these were not the same kinds of Blacks that lived in North Philly. At that time, I couldn't imagine that my parents would move me to a place where I would be in close proximity to people who were "dangerous." As a middle school student I heard my grandfather confirm those expectations when he explained that there were "niggers" and then there were "respectable Black people," and the ones in my class were most likely the respectable kind.

We were just kids, and we all loved each other like siblings. We laughed a lot and played together; we wrote plays and acted them out; we had kickball tournaments and tried to teach each other how to do back flips. I still remember (and still keep in touch with) many of the children from this elementary school.

I was just as close with the Black children as the White children. I remember being paired with Mark Samuels for square dancing. My immediate reaction was nervousness because he was Black. I had no other assumptions about race except that I worried that being paired with a Black partner would make me untouchable somehow; I had a crush on another boy from class. At that age I couldn't see anything wrong with Mark—I actually liked him quite a bit—but I knew deep inside that other kids and adults would perceive me differently if I let them know I liked Mark and the other children in my class who were Black.

## High School

I attended a predominantly White, middle-class, Catholic high school. My family was still struggling financially, and I qualified for free or reduced-lunch throughout my school years. At the high school I attended there were students from very wealthy families and students from middle-class families and a few of us who were definitely among those with the most limited financial resources.

Some of my friends from elementary and middle school also attended my high school, but many went to the local public high school. My school's racial and ethnic diversity was very limited, and this was glaringly obvious during every lunch period, when the small number of Black and Hispanic students all sat together at one table in the lunchroom. If you wanted to talk to one of them you had to visit that table. This is something I did often because of my friendship with several of the girls and guys and because of my unnoticed crush on Victor Lamas. I actually had never known anyone of Hispanic decent before I met Victor. He was so handsome and confident. He seemed at ease with everyone, and I liked the idea of being close to him.

Even though I took a lot of pride at the time in what I considered to be my "color blindness," I definitely held some misconceptions about other races and had never had anyone challenge my ideas. In fact, many prejudices and stereotypes were reinforced in the classrooms as well as at home. I was in honors courses with only one non-White student. Once I asked my grandmother what she thought about my going to the prom with one of my Black friends, and she said she would disown me. I asked her, "Really, you're kidding. You would really never talk to me again?" And she said, "Yes, I would miss you, but I would disown you."

What I had learned at home came crashing down on me like an avalanche one day while talking with Craig, an African American friend of mine, about the MOVE people in Philadelphia. MOVE was an organization of people who all took the last name "Africa." They believed in "Natural Law" rather than man-made laws, promoted clean environmental practices and ending suffering and oppression, and were primarily (if not all) African American.

The movement's back-to-nature philosophy meant that they did things like compost their waste. Neighbors began complaining about piles of compost and other things they perceived as health hazards. No one seemed to take the time to really get to know or listen to one another. As a result, an entire residential block in Philadelphia became headline news, and everyone was talking about it. Craig and his brother were my friends; we laughed and talked daily. One day in homeroom we talked about the MOVE issue.

Craig and I talked about how he didn't understand what was going on in Philly with this group. I started what I thought would be a point of agreement between the two of us. I explained the difference between niggers and regular, good Black people—I actually used those words. I immediately perceived this was the wrong thing to say and explained that he was a "good Black person," not a nigger. Craig's face changed. He was still facing me, but it was as if he couldn't see me anymore. More than 20 years later I remember the look on his face and still feel the humiliation of saying what I said.

## Next Stages

After college and a very short stint as a classroom teacher I decided to return to school and pursue my master's degree. I literally opened a *US News and World Report,* found the top five schools for education, and applied. As I perused their catalogues I could see that "risk and resilience" and "urban contexts" were the hot topics at these schools. I remember relating the concepts to my own life and feeling I might have something to offer.

Although I had definitely grown up with the privilege of being White, I didn't recognize that at all. I saw only the obstacles I had faced—low socioeconomic circumstances, family dysfunction, gender issues—and wondered why I had been so resilient in the face of those challenges. That prompted me to wonder what made anyone resilient in the face of obstacles, and that question ultimately became my platform as I applied to graduate schools.

Unable to see my own privilege, even as I began coursework at an Ivy League institution, I began to participate in the discourse around race and privilege. I took every chance to mention how hard life had been for me and how I had persevered—what was stopping someone else, just because they had brown skin? In my African American Psychology class I remember challenging the notion that Chris Rock could make fun of White folks but it was not okay for Whites to make fun of Blacks in the same way. With that remark at least a dozen brown faces turned to look at me. I immediately saw eyes roll and faces contort and heard mumbling. I knew my comment had not gone over well. In fact, it seemed clear that several of my classmates were visibly angry and insulted.

"Oh no, I can't even believe what I am hearing," Edith spoke up, and others agreed.

"But wait," I added. "Isn't this a double standard? Chris Rock can do a nerd character and play that as if it is the reality for all White men, and Chris Rock can do a horribly disrespectful bit about Black men, but if a White comedian does a Black character it's racist."

"Yes, yes, that's right!" Edith said.

I knew at that moment I was alone. All of a sudden the professor spoke up and said, "Now wait a minute. It's a fair comment, and it should be addressed with respect." For a moment I thought he was going to agree with me, and I was feeling kind of pumped and proud that I had spoken up. "If you disagree with her comment," he added, "explain why you disagree."

Marcia jumped in, "Okay, look. It's an in-group thing. If Chris Rock makes fun of Blacks it's okay because he is Black. If you make fun of Blacks, it is not—get it?"

*Not really*, I thought. But what I said was, "Okay, I'm sorry." I felt completely humiliated. In that moment I considered never going back to that class. I tried to explain my motives: "I've just thought about this issue a lot and thought I would ask."

"Well now you have the Black perspective—happy?" Edith retorted.

With that, the conversation ended, along with my verbal participation in that class. I did the reading and the work and enjoyed the class. However, it did not feel like a safe space for me to share anything that I didn't know for sure would be accepted by the group. This was a disappointing realization. That class became a place where I received information that I was not allowed to interrogate verbally. It forced a lot of self-reflection that was valuable. Still, it seemed like my classmates and I could have grown more if there had been an open dialogue.

During my second semester I was working at a research center and was in my seventh month of working as a classroom volunteer in a Head Start program. I had taken lots of classes, worked with children, and witnessed a shooting, so I felt that I was fully educated. Then during a staff meeting at the research center I referred to the children as "poor." The director immediately asked me to clarify what I meant by "poor children." It was clear from her pause and audible huff that she was displeased with me. I clarified that I was referring to their socioeconomic status. She asked that I use the term *low-resource* in lieu of *poor*.

To everyone else around the table it probably didn't seem like a big deal. Embarrassed and angry, I felt like I should explain to everyone that I grew up with limited resources so I knew what that was like. On the other hand, as little as I may have had sometimes, it was clear that my circumstances had not been those of the children I was working with. I had never feared for my safety walking to and from school, yet I knew these children did. I had never gone to school hungry, but many of my students did. I always had clean clothes and was bathed, but quite a few of my students did not have someone at home washing their clothes and making sure they took baths. And the worst assumption anyone ever made about me was simply that I was a spoiled rich kid because I was a White girl in a graduate program at an Ivy League school. I was always offended by that assumption, but I could not relate to my Black classmates—some of whom had prestigious undergraduate degrees and idyllic family backgrounds—who were assumed to be shoplifting whenever in a store, or presumed to be unintelligent or street-smart, even if they grew up in the suburbs.

## Continued Growth

It has been almost 15 years since those first few months of graduate school. Since then my own cultural identity has evolved over and over again. I have clear memories of the chip that was once on my shoulder.

I believe the biggest parts of my growth have come because of the relationships I have developed with friends who had different backgrounds from mine. These close relationships provide the safe space not available in other contexts. We share our own backgrounds, experiences, goals, and beliefs with one another. Through my friendships I have been able to confront my own assumptions and misunderstandings. In addition, I have been able to tell my story and be heard and understood.

The other important variable that has contributed to my growth has been working in schools and building relationships with the children in those schools. I worked with 4-year-olds in Head Start programs and teenagers in Philadelphia high schools. During my first year at a Head Start program my brother came to volunteer one day. About midday I noticed he was sitting on the floor in front of the bookcase. He had children all over him as he read books. One little boy, Omar, interrupted him and asked, "Are you White?"

My brother said, "Yes," to which Omar replied, "No, you can't be; you're so nice."

I think it was that moment that made me realize that our segregated society is the biggest culprit in misunderstanding and prejudiced actions. No one is immune to "isms" of any sort if we remain isolated from one another.

Even today, I find myself wanting to tell the story of what I didn't have in an effort to disown the privilege that I so obviously had by just having White skin. I often feel as if I am on a constant journey to understand both privilege and racism. I realize that in some contexts I am the oppressed and in others I have the power to be the oppressor. I must be aware of when I have the opportunity to use my unearned privilege to act with justice.

The dissonance this currently creates in my family is extremely difficult. On the one hand I feel it is a social justice issue, that when I hear or see behavior that is hurtful to someone (including me) it is my responsibility to speak up, to educate. On the other hand, this is my family. With every conflict I risk a lacuna that could be irreparable. Still, I try to challenge the status quo in our family when I can.

Humor carries a lot of capital in our family, and I have learned to use it well. For instance, just recently one of my uncles explained to me how he's "a real Jew about some things," in reference to his trying to save money. I didn't want to embarrass him and yet didn't want to let it go, so I used humor to bring attention to his words. He admitted that he is just in the habit of saying certain things without even considering the words he uses. So I confronted the issue, and it turned out okay, but I was actually terrified it would end up in conflict and hurt feelings.

Some members of my family do not recognize their privilege at all. They feel that they are oppressed. They have limited resources and have been affected by job loss and lack of formal education. It seems impossible for some of them to imagine that just being a White, heterosexual male carries privilege even when they are struggling to make ends meet. To be sure, to them my ideas sometimes seem foreign and delusional.

Now my struggle is to manage the resentment my family sometimes feels when I bring up issues of power and privilege while remaining truthful to what I have come to understand about them. This is difficult because now I see and hear things from those whom I love that I never heard before. It wasn't that racist remarks weren't being made before. It was just that I didn't hear them because they were part of my script also. On the other hand, I do understand how they feel oppressed by some of the aspects of their culture, and I want to respect their reality as well.

In the end, I can both maintain my feelings about privilege and power and continue to grow in the way I feel is right for me. I can respect the journey that those I love are on. The dialogue goes on in every phase of my life but continues to enrich my life and give me hope.

## Journal Questions

1. Find a picture of Puja (that is, how she looks in your imagination) and paste it into your journal; if you can't find one, draw one in your journal. Write down words about what you see, hear, smell, touch, and taste as you look at the picture. Then write about how she is and/or isn't exotic to you.

2. Tabitha has a childhood story of a Black man who held her at the welfare office. She uses that story as a touchstone to affirm that she is not inherently racist. Reflect on her thinking for four or five minutes, searching inside yourself for your own story that shows you are not inherently racist, then immediately flow write in your journal.

3. In your journal write the question, "What really matters?" Now think about Tabitha's experience in her graduate class when Edith said to her, "Now you have the Black perspective—happy?" What really matters about that experience? Think it over and then start writing.

4. Tabitha writes,

> I believe the biggest parts of my growth have come because of the relation-ships I have developed with friends who had different backgrounds from mine. These close relationships provide the safe space not available in other contexts. We share our own backgrounds, experiences, goals, and beliefs with one another. Through my friendships I have been able to confront my own assumptions and misunderstandings. In addition, I have been able to tell my story and be heard and understood.

Meditate on this quote in your own way (sitting or walking) for a few minutes, then write about it in your journal. Read your entry. What's going on in your body? Flow write about what you feel.

*Sharon J. Barnett at the time she was teaching in 2002*

# II

## THE MYTH OF THE LONE HERO

How a School in Brooklyn Taught
Me to Stay With a Broken Heart

*Sharon J. Barnett*

"I mainly wanted to save them, from poverty and hopelessness, and in the process figured I would be saved as well—from hopelessness, from fear. The fear that I didn't matter and couldn't, no matter how hard I tried, make a difference; that maybe people were right, that the divide in this country is too wide and the chances for these kids are too slim."

I remember afternoon sunlight streaming through the high, dirty windows along the west side of the classroom. After the kids left I would sit behind my teacher's desk and zone out, feeling the buzz of their energy draining from the room. I recall wanting time to stand still, willing the next moment, the next day, not to come. I would drift off, staring at the sunlight, recalling my life just a few months prior, before I had taken this job and stepped into a parallel universe. I would gather my things and set out for the long journey to my sublet on the border of Carnegie Hill and Spanish Harlem in Manhattan, high on the Upper East Side, one bus and two train rides away from this middle school in Bedford-Stuyvesant, Brooklyn. *Do-or-Die Bed-Stuy*, the kids called it, quoting the rapper The Notorious B.I.G. I knew nothing about the history of Bed-Stuy when I arrived.

When I traveled back and forth between the school and the subway station it looked like a warzone, the bus bumping along hole-pocked streets lined by abandoned buildings—broken windows, empty lots, and blowing trash. And no White folks. I was usually the only White person on the subway by the time we got to my stop.

Ninety-four percent of the children at the middle school where I was teaching were Black, and the remaining 6 percent were Latino. The only other Whites I saw in the halls of the school were teachers, and there weren't many of them—two, maybe three. Ms. Parnell, one of the other White teachers, would come swinging into my classroom during lunch, wearing baggy jeans and sneakers and bouncing on the balls of her feet like she was ready to run. Or fight. Her advice to me as a novice teacher: "Make them fear you. Close the doors to the classroom and refuse to let them go home at the end of the day. Use your cell phone and call guardians right in front of all the kids."

"Guardians?" I had asked. "You mean their parents?"

"Oh, 47 percent of these kids are in foster care and the rest don't necessarily live with their mother or father," she said casually. *Foster care? Forty-seven percent?* She went on: "Mock them. Get tough. Lose it. And above all: Make them fear you."

I may not be tough, but I had been raised to finish what I started. Failure was not an option. These were just kids who happened to be Black and brown and poor. They couldn't help where they happened to land in society. All they needed was someone like me, someone who recognized that they had gotten a raw deal in life but who could see them for who they really were. These kids had lost not one, but two, permanent teachers by the time I came to them in October, and I decided that I had to be the one who was going to stay. These kids had tested the hell out of those other teachers who resigned, but I knew they took it personally when those teachers left. I wanted to protect them from another experience of rejection.

Then I discovered that these kids didn't want me to rescue them. I didn't know anything about what it meant to survive and grow up in Do-or-Die Bed-Stuy. What I did have was 35 to 40 children turning up in my classroom or the outside hall every 90 minutes.

They showed up stoned, exhausted, or wired. Fights were common, teachers' cars outside were trashed, guns were waved around on a couple of occasions, and I had a child nearly strangled to death in the middle of my classroom by two grown men who ran in from off the street. If things got "out-of-hand," the principal advised me, threaten to hold the children after school. She said to make them fear me, just as Ms. Parnell had suggested.

The principal also informed me that sending students to her office was not an option. If I really needed assistance, she told me, I could send a child to find security. (The phones in the classrooms were broken, as were the metal detectors.)


## Cautious Revelations

This particular school and the children I encountered there are not representative of all of Black America. And I want to ensure I am not positioning myself as the victim here. However, I feel that there is something to be gained by sharing these profoundly painful experiences in my life because, you see, this is a story that documents the most significant—and heretofore-secret—failure of my adult life.

Because the dominant cultural story in which I have been raised ties my value and self-esteem to my capacity to be strong, capable, and above all, in control, admitting that I failed leaves me feeling rather exposed. As a White, middle-class woman the proper place for unpleasant business such as failure is in the closet—not in public, and *never* in view of strangers.

The mornings were easiest, when the children were groggy and hunched over their desks, willing to attempt whatever assignment I may have in store for them. Many were too tired to keep their eyes open or would busy themselves with brown sacks from the corner store where they had bought some kind of food item or drink that passed for breakfast. They were often distracted by what had happened the night before—a fight, a party, a hook-up. By the afternoon, they were in a frenzy. Sugar and boredom were a potent mix for these preadolescents; they bounced off the walls, at times quite literally.

Other mornings, when too few teachers had turned up for the day, we were informed that the children would be held in the auditorium for an unspecified period of time. I would stand around "guarding" the doors, and a movie would start—something ridiculous you'd rent on a Friday night from the local video store because they were out of anything good. Some of the children would sleep, but most would be restless and bored and pop up like kernels from their seats to throw something or shout out.

At the first of these assemblies I experienced, I remember the principal grabbed a megaphone and shouted threats at the students for daring to move. I was confused, thinking, *How are the children going to learn sitting in an auditorium for hours on end?* My confusion shifted to outrage. "Can I call the news channel and get the word out about this abuse?" I whispered to another teacher, Ms. Bailey. She just shrugged and said she'd tried that but had received no response.

## One Giant Leap

I always thought I would be a teacher. It felt not so much like a career choice as a calling. My first official teaching gig was when I was 12 years old. I taught Sunday School at Silvan Wesleyan Church in a small, predominantly White farming community about 20 miles outside of Melbourne, Australia. I was responsible for 15 to 20 children, ranging in age from four to eight. I was an optimistic preadolescent and structured my classroom hour down to the last minute. When chaos broke out, we moved on to the next activity, or when that didn't work, I broke into song. When *that* didn't work, I resorted to time-outs. But the moments of desperation were few and far between. I had boundless energy and recall grinning with pride when they all stood up to perform "This Little Light of Mine," hand motions included, in front of the congregation. Nothing could be better, I recall thinking, than inspiring kids. This was *it*.

My fourth-grade teacher, a White man named Mr. Hunter, was my absolute idol. He loved teaching, and as a consequence, we loved him. I felt like a genius in his class and wrote a 10-page book report on *The Hobbit*, despite the assignment's calling for something like 2 or 3 pages. I wanted to impress him. I wanted to *be* him. He was creative and entertaining and rigorous.

In high school, I continued to study my favorite teachers, each one White, keeping their outlines and my notes so that I could refer to them one day when I was a teacher. Whatever grade level I was at and class I was enjoying, I thought that must be the grade and subject I would teach. In grade 9, it was history, thanks to Ms. Smith. And in grades 11 and 12, it was modern history, thanks to Mr. Hamilton. It was thanks to him that I was slated to begin Asian studies at the University of Queensland. His interest had become mine, and I was eager to follow in his footsteps. I imagined returning someday to teach in my high school in a suburb of Brisbane.

How, then, did I end up teaching in Brooklyn, New York?

I had changed continents, thanks to my parents' decision that our family return to the nation of my birth after an absence of 12 years. I had also changed majors from education to history, mostly because my fascination with the turbulent political history of nations, thanks to Mr. Hamilton and Ms. Smith, had not waned.

Despite my change in major, teaching remained a constant. I taught cello in various schools and church basements. I tutored. I worked for Teachers on Call, a substitute staffing service, and saw the inside of many a preschool and child-care center. And I still wanted to teach when I graduated.

My last inspirational teacher had been at the university level, and I thought what I needed to do was obtain my doctorate. But the last thing I wanted to do was go straight into grad school. I wanted to *live* my life, not *read* about it. Plus, I had the small matter of my unconventional love interest looming large in my vision. Not only had I fallen in love with a woman, I had fallen in love with a Black woman. My head was spinning, my heart was pounding, and I knew I had to leap if I was ever going to figure this out.

Leaping appeared to be my MO. I had leapt from the rural, conservative, fundamentalist college of my parents' choosing to a large, urban public university. I had leapt from Sunday morning services and an engagement to a respectable, kind man to weekday protests as part of University Young Women. So why not leap again? This time I landed exactly where I felt I belonged.

After a year of "living," I decided it was time to return to pursuing what I felt was inevitable, my original calling: teaching. So, I enrolled in a postbaccalaureate teaching certification program. I was excited. I was enthused. There was no doubt in my mind that teaching was it. And so I began my program. Then came the moment that changed everything: my partner was accepted into a prestigious law school in New York. The Ivy League beckoned, and she wanted to answer the call. I knew what this meant for her and what I thought it meant for us. This was the big time.

So, just a few credits short of completing my program, I leapt again—but this time not alone. My love interest had blossomed into a full-blown relationship. In a U-Haul and with two cats in tow, my love and I headed east. She, to the beginning of what would become a successful international law career, and I, to a school in Brooklyn. Eventually, I obtained a position at the university working with a professor on designing and implementing a course to meet the emotional and social needs of undergraduate engineering students. I loved it, but it was not a permanent position.

At the end of my year, I was ready to return to my original calling: the classroom. At least, that's the part of the story I tell. The whole truth is that my love and I were drifting apart. In what was perhaps a last-ditch effort to keep my partner, I took the job as a teacher in the public middle school in Bedford-Stuyvesant, Brooklyn. I was close to being certified in Minnesota and thought I could at least sub while finishing up credits toward certification in New York.

I was offered a "permanent substitute" position in a school as an unlicensed teacher, and we needed the money. My partner had recently started exploring new facets of her Black identity, so this appeared to be an opportunity to prove to her that I could be tough, walk into situations that other White people thought were scary, and hold my own. Here was my chance to show her that I could do something grand.

I had been brought up to think of myself as racially neutral and to not notice racial realities. I did not see then that the legacy of racism is structured into our education system in a complex way—in funding, zoning, and taxes. That while I, like most White Americans, value ideas of individual achievement and equal opportunity, these kids are members of families and communities. Although their background does not completely determine their life path, these children, like me, are affected by the ranking or status of their group. Individual responsibility—mine or these children's—cannot replace the opportunities that only educational and economic structures can supply. If I had possessed such awareness would I have tried to take this on? And would I have tried to take it on *alone*?

## Control Your Class, Ms. Barnett

Two days into my new position, I realized the absurdity of my task. I recognized that I was grossly unprepared and suddenly wondered if I could just quit now, quietly, before the whole thing began. But it already felt too late. I had already met my classes. I had already purchased some books and materials. I had already called my family to tell them I had a job. My partner had already headed to upstate New York.

The original plan had been that we would be in the city together, but for logistical reasons and because of the conflicts we were starting to have, we thought it would be good to have a little distance and see each other on weekends. Now I was alone. I was new to the city, new to the job, and far too proud to call anyone for help.

I had numerous small victories during the day: moments of quiet while I read aloud to the children from our class novel; kids shouting out comments about what we had just read; kids struggling with writing assignments;

students sharing with me the raps they wrote on their own time. But to me these moments were simply what was supposed to be happening in a classroom; I didn't recognize them for the small miracles they were.

What I did notice were the fights—the times when, unbeknownst to me, some threat had been hurled and suddenly everyone was on their feet, desks thrown aside, while two girls removed their rings and then ran at each other, the class shouting from the sidelines. And then the principal would come through the door screaming at the children, then screaming at me, "Control your class, Ms. Barnett! What's wrong with you?"

One morning a child threw a glass bottle across the classroom only to have it shatter inches from the trash can, the intended destination. At that moment, the principal just happened to be walking by our room, a rare occurrence. She heard the shattering glass and came storming in, glared at me, and began screaming at the kids. Once she learned who the offender was she ordered the child to pick up the glass *and hurry*. The offender was a meek, bespectacled girl named Laketta. She was shy and sweet and usually did everything she could not to be noticed. My heart went out to her as she received the principal's rage, and when she cut her fingers on the glass, I had to intervene.

The principal told me in no uncertain terms to be quiet and told the girl to keep picking up the glass, even as blood trickled down her hand to her wrist. Shaking with rage, I walked out of the classroom and into the hallway where I leaned against the wall. I tried to take deep breaths, but I was screaming *NO* so loudly in my head, I could barely do that. I wanted to walk away, I wanted to rail against the principal, I wanted, I wanted . . . what? What could I do? I was simultaneously furious and terrified. Powerless.

I felt like I had no control over my situation or the strength of my fury. All I could do was stand there and quake. Fury had always turned to silence for me. I could never lash out in rage. So I waited, loathing myself for not having the courage to stand up for Laketta and cursing my inability to walk away altogether so as not to participate in this injustice. What adult lets a child be hurt in her presence? A weak one. A scaredy cat. A fool. My rage simmered down once I found a recipient I *could* lash out at: myself. Suddenly soothed, I walked back into the room, ignoring both the principal and Laketta. The class was silent as she continued picking up the glass, as the blood continued to trickle down and drip onto the floor.

The principal was African American, so this behavior was perplexing to me. Race, racism, prejudice—these were all simple concepts in black-and-white. White people had done wrong to Black people. *We* were the offenders.

*They* were in need of saving from historical and present-day injustice. But *this*? I could not fathom the internal workings of the principal or her right-hand man, the assistant principal, also African American. Were they good soldiers for some higher-up authority, held to demands that were unreasonable, accountable for outcomes over which they did not have the resources to control? I spent less time thinking about them critically than I did scheming about how to stay off their radar. Look away. Don't ask for help. Keep the kids in the classroom at all costs.

Emotionally, I felt like a child trying to avoid a tyrannical, abusive parent. Nothing I did felt good enough. Like a child, I did not outwardly question any of these demands. I was in survival mode. My primitive brain screamed flight, but I froze. I returned each day to that school like some kind of zombie, resigned to my fate. I shut down and went through the motions: up in the dark, a half-eaten bowl of cereal and two cups of coffee, an hour's commute, and then a day divided into 60-minute and 45-minute blocks. In the middle somewhere was a lunch break during which I would attempt to eat something, anything, to get me through the rest of the day.

I was doing what I had been socialized to do as a good White woman: suffer silently, turn the rage inward, and strive for perfection. Resent those around you for not seeing your suffering, but don't ask for help. *Never* ask for help. To ask for help is to admit weakness, to admit that you—*gasp!*—have needs. Let the resentment grow. I kept my struggles to myself.

I began craving a drink in the evening as I wrote my lesson plans. I vacillated between seeing these children as depraved villains and heroic victims. Here were these kids, I recall thinking, living their lives with such bravery and bravado, and I was coming home each night to my safe, tiny cocoon of an apartment and drinking gin. I was also frustrated and confused to see that others, other Whites and African Americans, seemed able to do what I was finding increasingly difficult: show up.

These other people at the school fell primarily into two camps. There were the Christians who appeared to be motivated by a desire to save these kids' souls and were less concerned with academic achievement. And then the others: people who were "doing time" and not afraid to express their opinion that we were just a holding place for these kids who were bound for jail or the streets.

I was scared to come too close to the Christians out of my discomfort with their perspective and out of fear that they would reject me for being queer. And I was appalled by the stance of the others who appeared to despise these children. I didn't want to approach these kids with condescension or hopelessness. I wanted to show up with . . . what? I wasn't sure at the time. I mainly wanted to save them, from poverty and hopelessness, and in the process figured I would be saved as well—from hopelessness, from fear. The fear that I didn't matter and couldn't, no matter how hard I tried, make a difference; that maybe people were right, that the divide in this country is too wide and the chances for these kids are too slim. The pain of that possibly being true was too much to face.

One teacher, an African American woman named Ms. Bailey, was different. She both loved these kids and was able to teach them. They mostly settled down in her class and adored her. They even did some work for her. I would meet with her as often as I could, but she was exhausted and coping with health issues, so I didn't want to burden her with my struggles. She would lift one eyebrow when I'd show up at her door and say, "Well, Ms. Barnett, how's it going?" And I would fight back tears, pretending everything was okay.

One afternoon, there's some commotion in the hallway. I tell some kids to get to their classrooms, and the next thing I know I'm on the ground, holding onto someone's baseball cap. I'm confused but stand up and see that the kids have dispersed and the vice principal is walking toward me. He takes my arm and escorts me to the principal's office a few doors down.

I feel like I'm underwater. The principal is speaking, but I can't quite make out what she's saying. I try to come up for air, but I can't, so I just sit there and try to make sense of her muffled tones. The next thing I know a boy, the owner of the baseball cap, is being escorted into the office. He's being told to say he is sorry and he does this, looking not the least bit sorry, and then is told to sit outside the office while I make my decision.

Decision? I shake my head, hoping it will shake off the liquid that has replaced my brain. Decision? The principal looks at me like I'm an idiot and apparently repeats what she has been saying all along: The owner of the baseball cap is on parole. If I say the word, his parole office gets called and he goes off to prison. This is his last chance. Even though he is in the eighth grade, he is 18 years old and he has done much worse than pushing a teacher down in the hallway, but no matter: Say the word and he's gone.

"Me? Say the word?" I say stupidly.

"Yes," she says. "This is assault. Or, you could just forgive him and he'll go back to class." She then goes on to remind me that we are simply a holding cell for these kids who are bound for jail or janitorial work. "So," she says, summing up her point, "does he go now or later?" She steps outside her office and walks the boy back in to stand him in front of me. She tells him that I have made my decision. I can barely get the words out, but somehow manage to say, "it's okay" or something to that effect.

The boy takes my hand and smiles coyly, "Thank you, Ms. Barnett."

I look at the principal and she looks away, then says, "Don't you have a class to teach?"

And then I walk away.

## Broken Promise

I admitted the truth of my situation to a close friend over the telephone— what really went on at the school and how I was responding—and at her insistence I left. I had lasted longer than the three previous teachers in my position, but it didn't matter. All I knew is that I had made a promise to myself and to these kids and that I had broken it.

I was the teacher who was there for school photos. I was the teacher who told them—*out loud*—I would not be leaving. I was the teacher who tried to inspire, who read aloud from funny and interesting books, who spent entire paychecks on compelling reading materials for the class, who talked with them about possibilities and about other places far from the streets where they lived. How do I convey how crucial it felt for me to stay? How do I convey the many strands of my life that came together to create this moment in which it felt both impossible to go and impossible to stay?

You see, I had started by wanting simply to do what I had always wanted to do: teach. But I had also desperately wanted to prove to my soon-to-be-ex that I was on her side. I wanted to atone for the color of my skin, for the privilege I never asked for but received daily, handed to me like a gift I could not refuse to take. I wasn't raised or educated in the United States until university, so I think I was also naïve; I didn't really *get* how deep the divide was between the educational experience of most White children and poor, urban, Black and Latino children.

I was worn down by the exhaustion of essentially creating my own curriculum, by 14-hour days, from my loneliness, from my fear of being screamed at and humiliated by the principal in front of other staff and the children I was striving to teach, and from my own moral angst over participating in a system that treated these children like inmates.

I made up a lie to the kids about my brother's needing me in Minneapolis. The lie was only a partial one, but I still felt sick as I told them. A few of

THE MYTH OF THE LONE HERO    151

them asked me if I'd been jumped and if that was the real reason I was leaving. I assured them it wasn't and fleshed out my story. I knew they could relate to needing to be there for a sibling in trouble, and I used that knowledge to my benefit.

I felt such shame, I didn't even say good-bye to Ms. Bailey. I just left, a little over four months after starting my position.

A few months later my partner and I decided to end our relationship. She kept her family and our friends in New York. I retreated to my home in Minneapolis. Suddenly my world was virtually all White. I couldn't bear to think or talk about my experience at the middle school in Brooklyn, and when I first returned to Minneapolis I wanted to avoid places that bore any resemblance to that time and place. I would start shaking just walking along the street when I heard booming bass from a car or passed large groups of Black folks hanging out on their front lawn.

I had gone from being an open-hearted person to acting like a scared White woman. Before teaching in Brooklyn I had worked and socialized with people of color. I had lived with a Black woman. I had celebrated holidays for years with my partner's family, large groups of Black and brown folk in which I was frequently the only White person present. But given my fear and my paranoid thoughts, I was left with what seemed to me a very reasonable conclusion: I was just another scared White liberal whose sentimental fantasies for closing the racial divide had been shattered. When it came to race and connection, I was clearly a failure, personally *and* professionally.

## New Lessons Learned

Years later I found myself in a classroom again, this time as a student learning how to become "culturally competent." Imagine my surprise when the professor immediately drew our attention to our bodies, saying our work is to keep our nervous system open, to stay receptive to new and uncomfortable information. She spoke of two different intelligences, cognitive and somatic, and said that we would be drawing on both with an emphasis on the latter. Furthermore, she said, those of us who didn't have skills of emotional regulation might have difficulty receiving the content of this class. I was intrigued. This was a class about race and culture, and she was talking about the body and emotion.

I remember starting to feel excitement and panic as it began to dawn on me that I would be unable to avert my eyes from my private pain if I wanted to truly participate in this class. She said something about a tendency to blame ourselves when we act or think in ways we don't like—a tendency we have because of our culture's focus on the individual. This focus neglects to see the power of context, and so, she said emphatically, be kind to yourself as you notice how you've been powerfully shaped by cultural and familial relationships.

I was moved by her use of the word "kind." Could I really relate with kindness to the naïve woman who took that job in Brooklyn, New York? And what about letting go of blame—blame for the ways I contributed to the end of my relationship, blame for walking away from my classes of kids who needed someone to be there for them, blame for my secret desire to simply ignore racism and its effects—could I really let that go?

It was starting to come together in that very first class: If responding with kindness is so terribly difficult, is it any wonder that I don't want to move toward this pain and confusion? Is it any wonder that I keep myself out of situations where I might have to look at this suffering? That I avoid people and places that might trigger these painful thoughts and feelings?

Perhaps the most radical piece of information I received about relating skillfully to emotions was the idea of learning to "be comfortable with being uncomfortable." Rather than responding in our habitual ways to discomfort—assuming something is wrong, assuming we have to change what we're doing—we were offered the challenge to lean in, get closer, foster an attitude of curiosity. Learning this information about how to relate skillfully to my emotions was allowing me to take in race-related content like I had never been able to do before. This content was causing me to re-vision my past, my family, my way of looking at all the forces that were at play in my relationship, the middle school in Brooklyn, and how I related to them. I could take in this information and not be hijacked by the difficult emotions that were triggered by the horrors of racism and the reality of my participation in it.

The more soothed I felt, the more open I was to seeing the fear and judgment in my heart. I continue to realize over and over again: I have to see something before I can let it go. Once known, I can make a choice *not* to act from a place of fear or judgment. I can choose to bring in wisdom and act from that place.

## Coming Full Circle

I returned to a public school setting last year for the first time since walking out of the middle school in Bed-Stuy, and this time I returned as a therapist, not a teacher. It felt like a good fit to be working one-on-one with children and addressing their emotional needs. At this urban elementary school with mostly Black and Latino students I was at times reminded of my time in Bed-Stuy, but the differences were stark, not just in the school setting but within myself. This time I had the education, training, and support to do what I was doing. I certainly did not go it alone.

I felt like I was coming full circle, doing the work I wish I could have done back then, seeing these kids in the full context of their lives and feeling equipped to do effective work. Had it not been for my time in Bed-Stuy, it's possible I would have approached these kids with some of the same misapprehensions I had held at the time: that our differences in race (and class) don't matter, that I've figured out exactly what they need, and that I can on some level "rescue" them.

My desire to teach has not entirely left me; I feel it every time I have the opportunity to train new therapists. I suppose I feel the same way I did as a child—that teaching is more of a calling and less of a career choice—and because that's so, it's probably just a matter of time before I return to the classroom as a teacher.

## Journal Questions

1. In your journal write the following headline: "Sharon Barnett Fails in Her Adult Life!" Flow write the rest of the story.

2. Begin your journal with the words, "There was no doubt in my mind teaching was it. I knew . . ." and continue to write.

3. After an experience with a bespectacled girl name Laketta and a principal, Sharon writes, "I wanted to walk away, I wanted to rail against the principal, I wanted, I wanted . . . what? What can I do? I was simultaneously furious and terrified. Powerless." Have a 10-minute huddle with your "inner coach" about Sharon's predicament. Write down your coach's wisdom. What did you learn?

4. Sit down with your journal, take several deep breaths, and then write Sharon a condolence letter.

## References

hooks, b. (2000). *All about love: New visions.* New York: Harper Perennial.

Karis, T. A. (2002). *Racial mindfulness: A foundation for creating connection in relationships.* Unpublished manuscript.

Karis, T. A. (2007, September 11). University of Wisconsin–Stout, Menomonie, WI. Lecture.

Lawrence, K., Sutton, S., Kubisch, A., Susi, G., & Fulbright-Anderson, K. (2004). Structural racism and community building. *Aspen Institute Roundtable on Community Change*. Washington, D.C.: The Aspen Institute.

Robb, C. (2006). *This changes everything: The relational revolution in psychology*. New York: Farrar, Straus and Giroux.

Walker, M. (1999). Race, self, and society: Relational challenges in a culture of disconnection. *Work in Progress, No. 85*. Wellesley, MA: Stone Center Working Paper Series.

# 12

# PAYING ATTENTION TO RACIAL MATTERS

## Personal and Professional Development

*Terri A. Karis*

"Although well intentioned, not paying conscious attention to race has significant drawbacks."

I n this book personal stories have been presented as a method for exploring experiences of race and difference. This chapter continues that exploration by offering ideas for continued professional and personal development on the topic of race. Becoming professionally skillful regarding racial matters requires starting right where we are. Some of us have paid a lot of attention to race and feel competent when thinking and talking about race. Many of us, however, feel hesitant, afraid we don't know enough about racial matters to express an opinion, afraid we might say the wrong thing and offend someone. This is a great place to begin. The stories in this book have provided us with examples of women bringing curiosity and the freshness of not knowing to the task of learning more about race. We can do this, too.

## Personal Awareness

When it comes to race, the foundation for professional and personal development is simply paying attention, with interest and curiosity. Those of us who are White typically have been socialized to not notice race, and to believe it is good and right to behave this way. We might assume that not attending to race is a way to put into practice our values of equality and respect for all people.

Although well intentioned, not paying conscious attention to race has significant drawbacks. First, attempting to ignore race is not the same as creating equality. Not noticing race leaves ongoing racial disparities intact and misses important aspects of life for those who continue to experience them. Second, a lack of conscious awareness about race results in being under the influence of the unconscious, implicit racial stereotypes that permeate American culture.

## How to Pay Attention

### *Mindful Awareness*

A foundation for race-related learning is "mindful awareness," the process of actively and openly observing our mental, emotional, and physical experiences moment by moment. Bringing conscious attention to whatever is going on supports our ability to self-regulate and face the discomfort that often accompanies race-related learning.

### *Become Comfortable With Being Uncomfortable*

As we pay attention to race, one of the first things we're likely to notice is that we feel uncomfortable. Confusion, hurt, anger, shame—none of us enjoys these feelings but sometimes they get triggered as we learn about race. Our challenge is not to let being uncomfortable stop us. With kindness and self-empathy we can draw on what we already know about how to stick with something, even when it is uncomfortable.

### *Use Feelings: There's More to Explore*

Uncomfortable feelings get our attention. Feelings are actually a useful indicator that there is more to explore. Rather than just trying to move away from them as quickly as possible, view them as a sign of having run up against a new idea that challenges a prior, perhaps unexamined, belief. We can cultivate curiosity about what we haven't yet discovered about ourselves and our own thinking habits.

### Let Go of Self-Judgment

As we notice patterned thinking and feeling responses it's not uncommon to judge what we see. When we become aware of self-judgments, our work is to hold them "loosely," or "lightly." In Kat Griffith's story (chapter 4), she demonstrates mindful awareness of self-judgment:

> I have moments in which I find them scary. I think guiltily, *Is this just my being racist? . . . Why am I afraid of these guys, and I'm not afraid of the White wrestlers and football players who also frequent the hall? . . .* I'm horrified that my feelings look like typical racist-White-person feelings.

Kat's example is useful because she doesn't let disturbing thoughts immobilize her or shut down the learning process. Harsh self-judgments often function as obstacles to continued engagement. Can we instead offer ourselves kind acceptance, even if we don't like what we see? We all have been shaped in different but predictable ways by living in a racially stratified culture. No one is free from racial stereotypes, and compassionately recognizing this is a starting place for working with our patterns.

### Stay With the Process

To deepen racial understanding requires a willingness to stay with the process and begin to reflect on and question our race-related thoughts, feelings, and behaviors. It can be uncomfortable to stay with the process of observing ourselves when what we see is undesirable. Seeing and naming honestly, without judgment, is still the foundation for continued learning. We can be interested in and curious about our own unwillingness. Whatever we encounter can become the path of continued engagement rather than becoming the dead end that shuts down the learning process.

## What to Pay Attention To

### Racial Moments

We can practice paying attention to race by noticing what I call "racial moments." A racial moment is simply whenever race comes into your awareness, and it can happen anytime—watching TV, talking with students, observing an interaction at the grocery store, reading a book. The following are the instructions I have used with students.

## Racial Moments Systematic Self-Observation

Go about your daily life as you normally do. When race comes into your awareness through a thought, feeling, or interaction please observe it. Don't change it, judge it, or do something different. Simply document the experience using the following format. It is helpful to document a racial moment as soon as possible after you notice it so that it is fresh in your awareness.

### *Reflection Questions*

1. What is the situation?
2. Who is involved? (It might be just you.)
3. What are the thoughts, feelings, and/or words spoken?
4. Reflection afterward: How do you understand what happened? What were your thoughts and feelings that came after the initial thoughts or feelings?

It is not essential to follow this format strictly, but it helps at first to have a structure that supports systematically paying attention. Our work is to notice the thoughts, feelings, and even body sensations present, and to relate to whatever we notice with friendly respect rather than judgment.

This observational practice goes beyond the questions "Am I racist?" and "Was what I just observed racist?" These questions organize attention in particular ways but may get in the way of seeing important aspects of race. The ways that we present ourselves and interpret others' behavior have been unconsciously shaped by cultural aspects of race. These ways of being in the world are perhaps most apparent when we're exposed to habits or behaviors different from our own, but from this cultural perspective race is being performed even when an all-White family is having dinner together or a White teacher is interacting with White students. Paying attention to racial moments is one tool for learning more about racial meanings and how we unconsciously perform our racial identities.

### *Racial Assumptions*

As we practice racial mindfulness we can bring awareness not only to our thoughts about race but also to the underlying assumptions we draw on as we interpret the world around us. In the following example Tara Affolter (chapter 8) names how her racial assumptions became visible as they changed.

> I never talked about these lessons [critiquing the racial dynamics of *To Kill a Mockingbird*] . . . because I didn't understand them for a while. It seemed

enough to have students on stage together, but I would soon learn that it was not nearly enough.

What if you don't have awareness of your own assumptions? Stick with the process of paying attention and you will discover more about your own mind.

## Unconscious Racial Preferences

One tool for learning more about our subconscious minds is the Implicit Association Test (IAT). This test measures unconscious (that is, implicit) bias about race, age, gender, and other variables. Even when we are not consciously thinking about race, our judgments and actions may be impacted by our "implicit mind." The following website offers the IAT as a tool for gaining greater awareness about unconscious preferences and beliefs.

http://implicit.harvard.edu/implicit/demo/measureyourattitudes.html

## Dominant Cultural Stories About Race

In addition to noticing our own assumptions we can pay attention to the racial "stories" told by other people and in movies, books, and the news. Although each individual has his or her own habitual thinking habits and assumptions, our stories mirror cultural patterns. One way to begin to notice more about race is to identify what Lee Anne Bell (2010) calls "stock stories"—dominant-culture stories about race.

By reading this book you've already taken a step in challenging one dominant cultural story about race: color blindness. Color blindness encourages not paying attention to race and how it shapes who we are, our personal interactions, and our schools. Although this behavior typically is based on good intentions, not paying attention results in maintaining the racial status quo.

When you hear or read something about race, you can pose questions to yourself: Does the story support color blindness—not paying attention to race—or color consciousness—paying attention? What is the person's understanding about why that particular approach is preferable?

You can also be on the lookout for two types of "counterstories" that challenge dominant stories and offer inspiration and encouragement. "Concealed stories" challenge stock stories by highlighting both the strengths of those in marginalized communities and the ways race shapes their lives.

"Resistance stories" tell how people challenge racial inequality and work for racial justice.

## Interpersonal Connections

All the personal work you do to become more aware of race-related thoughts and feelings lays the foundation for being more interpersonally skillful. Still, because a racially stratified culture is by definition a culture of disconnection, it is inevitable that we sometimes will experience disconnections regarding racial matters. Despite wanting to connect, one human being to another, all of us carry stereotypes that get in the way of clearly seeing others and ourselves. Stereotypes fuel fear and movement away from those we perceive as different, constraining what we think is possible in relationships with those across racial lines (and with those in our own racial category who hold different views). Noticing habits of disconnection, we can approach ourselves and others with kindness. We are not bad people but people who have been deeply socialized into patterns of disconnection. This is painful. Kindness and caring are essential to helping us face the pain of wanting to connect and not always knowing how.

### *Experiments in Interpersonal Racial Engagement*

*Open the door.*

Move toward talking about race rather than away from it. Many of us shy away from—or resolutely avoid—discussing race. From a place of genuine curiosity, can we experiment with opening the door to having conversations about race? We may not know yet what to say, but we can learn by asking questions, like "Tell me more about what you meant by . . ." If you hear something that you find offensive, rather than ignoring it or saying, "Don't talk that way around me," open the door to learn more: "Help me understand what's funny about that joke."

*Understanding, not agreement.*

Cultivate curiosity about how others experience difference. Listen—*really listen*—with a goal of understanding, not necessarily agreement. Numerous surveys report significant differences between how racial groups perceive issues. Can you stay open to hearing another's perspective without having to assess what is right or true? Because this is just an experiment, set your appraisal aside and make understanding your only goal. This experiment is also useful with those in your own racial group whose views you find irritating or intolerable. Be curious and learn about why they see things as they do. Can we do this without feeling superior because we're convinced our views are more conscious? Our job is not to change them but simply to understand the world from their perspective.

*Risk connecting across difference.*

Develop relationships with those you perceive as different. Start small and go slowly. Be on the lookout for people who interest you and be friendly. Say "hello" rather than avoiding contact. Strike up conversation about what's going on around you. Begin to frequent places where there is racial diversity. These behaviors may involve going outside the norms or "unspoken rules" of your particular group, and you will probably feel uncomfortable. Notice with kindness, and support yourself in continuing to stretch into new experiences.

*Bring more of yourself to the interaction.*

This experiment is useful when interacting with those in your own racial group who you wish would think or act differently. When you notice the impulse to try and change the other, or see yourself avoiding racial discussions because you've given up hope that they will ever change, try sharing more of yourself. Your goal is to talk about your own values or your own view rather than to change the other. Expressing our values, we participate in creating a world that reflects them and support others who share our values but may not yet have found their voices.

*Learn more about history.*

Knowing about the history of race relations provides a context for understanding others' behaviors. Without this knowledge, we increase the likelihood of making inaccurate interpretations about behaviors of those who are racially different. Having been socialized into thinking of people as simply individuals, we can experiment with considering how membership in a particular racial group might shape a person's experience. The following scenario and questions offer an example of how to explore multiple interpretations of an interpersonal interaction.

## Scenario Exploring How Race Shapes Interpersonal Interactions

In a racially mixed group, Paulette, a Black woman, talked about being the only non-White person attending a recent holiday gathering. She talked about her hurt and anger at (once again!) being mistaken for the maid. She went on to say that, when she was at gatherings where only one or two White people were present, she made a special point of making them feel comfortable. Almost immediately Wendy, a White woman, shared that she'd been at a gathering once where she was the only White person, and she hadn't felt very welcomed. Erica, a White woman, overheard this conversation and felt very uncomfortable with what Wendy had just said but didn't say anything.

## Reflection Questions

1. We can think about each woman as an individual. What is each woman feeling? Can you feel empathy for the experience each is having?

2. We can think about the race of each woman. How or in what ways does thinking about racial group membership change your interpretations about the interaction?

3. Is the experience Wendy described comparable to the experience Paulette described? How and in what ways is it similar? How and in what ways it is dissimilar?

4. What historical and cultural factors would support the view that Paulette's experience was actually quite different from Wendy's? If Wendy had been aware of these factors how might she have responded differently to Paulette?

5. What about this situation made Erica feel uncomfortable? What might have gotten in the way of her speaking?

6. What might Erica have said that would have helped her deepen her connection with Wendy? with Paulette?

7. How might this scenario be relevant to your work as a teacher?

## *The Benefit of Multiple Perspectives*

With all these experiments it is useful to share your thoughts and experiences with a friend, colleague, or small group who has a commitment to paying more attention to race. Creating nonjudgmental social connections supports us as we observe, question, and experiment with new ways of paying attention. It's important to see that we're not alone with our discomfort and not knowing. We can learn from others' ideas and mistakes, and feel calmed and reassured by sharing the learning process together.

## Parent-Teacher-Principal Scenario

(With thanks to Judith James, judithm474@earthlink.net)

You have an African American ninth grader, LeMar, in your sociology class. LeMar spends much of his class time joking around with other students, distracting the class with his antics, and disrupting class work. You have spoken to LeMar at length about the importance of his receiving credit in your class to be on track for graduation. When you speak with LeMar he is respectful and appears receptive to your concerns, but his behavior does not change. You have requested he stay after school to do homework with you, and for a couple days he does stay and receive tutoring. As you work together you realize he has a hard time comprehending the reading, and you make a referral to a remedial reading class. If LeMar understands the text he is quite adept at answering the assigned questions, but it is painful for him to read the text, even with your help. You have attempted to call a parent twice and there has been no return call. You send a note home with LeMar asking a parent to call you and giving a time when you can be reached; you have still received no communication from a parent.

By the fourth week of class LeMar is failing and continues to fall behind other students. In a team meeting it is decided that LeMar be removed from your class and put in a remedial reading class offered at the same time as your class. LeMar is disturbed by this news and angry that he cannot stay with his friends. The Tuesday after his first week in the remedial class you receive a note from the principal asking you to meet with him and LeMar's parent. You run into the principal in the hall. He lets you know LeMar's mother is angry and believes your actions are based on your racist attitudes toward students of color.

## *Reflection Questions*

Imagine yourself in this situation and explore the following questions:

1. What are your thoughts and feelings when you receive the principal's note? after you run into him in the hall? Is there anything you need to do to emotionally prepare for the meeting?

2. As you anticipate the meeting with the principal and LeMar's mother, what is your plan? Consider your objectives and what you hope for as the best possible outcome. What will you bring to the meeting? Who should be included? Will you ask that LeMar attend, or just meet with the principal and parent without him? What are the beliefs and assumptions that shape your choices?

3. Will you respond to the accusations of being racist, and if so, how?

The following paragraph offers one possible scenario for how this situation might unfold. This is *not* meant to suggest that there is only one right way to handle the situation, but is offered as a catalyst to stimulate your thoughts. As you read, notice your own thoughts and feelings. What catches your attention? What surprises you? Use these to become aware of possible blind spots. If you agree or disagree with how the teacher handles the situation, use either response to learn more about your own beliefs and assumptions. *If you want to maximize your learning, make sure you have answered the preceding questions before going on.*

Here is how a White female teacher in a large inner-city school handled the situation. First, she planned to bring her grade book and LeMar's assignments to the meeting. She also brought the textbook and highlighted places in the text where LeMar had trouble comprehending what he read. She had with her the reading specialist's evaluation stating LeMar was reading at a fifth-grade level and needed remedial assistance. Finally, she brought her extensive notes detailing LeMar's behavior in class. *These documents were her backup strategy.* The teacher knew that starting with them would create a hostile environment with LeMar's mother, and she knew that before talking about anything else she first had to make it clear to LaMar's mother that she cared about her son and had his best interests at heart. She also knew that somehow she would need to address the race issue.

What will her approach be in the meeting? *Before reading further, role-play the teacher's meeting with the parent and the principal. Noticing where you don't know what to do or say is useful information. Discuss any stuck spots with other colleagues.*

The following is one possible dialogue among the parent, teacher, and principal.

## One Possible Dialogue

Dr. Goodwill (Principal): Good afternoon, Ms. Johnson. I would like you to meet Mrs. Bernice Smith.

Mrs. Smith: Hello, Ms. Johnson. [*Mother is clearly angry and does not look at Ms. Johnson*]

Ms. Johnson: Welcome, Mrs. Smith. [*Ms. Johnson knows that at no time should she refer to Mrs. Smith as "Bernice," nor should she call her "Ms. Smith," unless the mother asks her to*]

Dr. Goodwill: Mrs. Smith and I have been talking about LeMar's behavior in your class and subsequent transfer to a remedial reading class. As you might imagine, she is upset with the move and wants an explanation.

At this point Ms. Johnson *could* say how she tried to get hold of Mrs. Smith several times with no apparent response and thinks Mrs. Smith should have called her back if she was concerned about her son. *But she will not.* Mrs. Smith may or may not have gotten those calls, but it will serve no purpose to bring them up because Ms. Johnson wants to align herself with Mrs. Smith.

Ms. Johnson: As you already know, Dr. Goodwill, and let me say at this time to Mrs. Smith, this was a very hard choice for me because I enjoy LeMar in class tremendously. He is such a sweet young man and has all the potential in the world, but just continued to fall behind the other students in his homework. I could not stand by and watch the painful experience he was going through as he tried to keep up with the reading without the required reading skills.

Mrs. Smith: [*Obviously agitated*] What do you mean he didn't have the reading skills? He has been in school for nine years. Why hasn't he learned to read?

Dr. Goodwill: That's an excellent question and understandably one that would make any parent angry. Why teachers or administrators in other buildings have passed him on without ensuring he was equipped to be successful we cannot address. What I will say is that we will not do that here.

Mrs. Smith: Like I haven't heard that before. Same old story. Put the blame on someone else. And my community wants to know why there is an achievement gap! This is why!

Dr. Goodwill: I hope you believe me, but I would understand why you wouldn't. We care about the achievement gap and are attempting to close it here at Mendota High. Your son is a good example of why we must put a stop to low achievement in all young people. He is a fine young man, has the potential for a college degree, and his education cannot be wasted by his antics.

Mrs. Smith: Antics! What antics? He is fine at home. The issue is that most of the teachers here, and you, Dr. Goodwill, are White. You don't understand our children, and your racism gets in the way of helping them.

Now Ms. Johnson gets out her written materials and makes a case for LeMar's needing remedial help, but first she addresses the race issue.

Ms. Johnson: [*With emotion but not defensiveness*] Mrs. Smith, of course we are all affected by racism, but I am not here to discuss my racism. I would be open to talking with you at a different time and place if that is a discussion you want to have with me. But I want our focus to be on LeMar. My racism is not the issue right now. What I want us to look at is what's affecting LeMar's reading comprehension. As you can see on this reading comprehension test he reads at a fifth-grade level.

Mrs. Smith: Yes.

Ms. Johnson: Well, like you, I want him to be successful. I assumed being in a class where he could improve his reading comprehension was the solution. And, by the way, we have found that in six months most students improve their comprehension by at least two grade levels. I am sorry I did not have a chance to talk to you beforehand [*Again, Ms. Johnson knows there is no need to mention she called unless the mother asks, but she knows she must make sure she has tried calling before ever getting to a meeting*], but I am open to other solutions you may have. You tell me what we can do. We cannot let LeMar leave this building without the possibility of going to college. [She does not say just "graduate"]

Mrs. Smith: Well, how long does he have to be in reading comprehension classes, Dr. Goodwill?

Dr. Goodwill: I would say for the rest of the year [six months] and three months in summer school. He should be at his grade level in reading by the 10th grade. What do you think, Ms. Johnson?

Ms. Johnson: I absolutely agree. This is a smart young man, and if you, Mrs. Smith, encourage him to be patient and seek extra help from his teachers, and let him know he will be able to go to college if he can successfully comprehend what he reads—and he can, I know he can—it will help us a lot.

## Reflection Questions

1. What were your thoughts and feelings about the dialogue?

2. How or in what ways is it a realistic conversation? How or in what ways is it not realistic?

3. What themes did Ms. Johnson stress throughout the conversation? What did she do to try and align herself with Mrs. Smith? What are your thoughts about her choices?

4. How did she handle the race issue? What are your thoughts about her choices? How would you have addressed Mrs. Smith's concerns about racism?

5. What do you imagine will happen to LeMar? How do you imagine Mrs. Smith felt after the conference?

## Structural Arrangements

Although personal awareness and interpersonal connections are important for understanding race, race is not just an internal psychological phenomenon. Because of the dominant stock story that we are "just" individuals, the interconnections between institutional arrangements, interpersonal relations, and personal identities often are invisible.

Several of the stories in this book highlight how personal awareness and interpersonal skillfulness were not sufficient to address the structural aspects of race. Creating change on this level may seem daunting; the following ideas are small steps for beginning to pay attention to this aspect of race. In the following section you will find learning activities that offer group opportunities for exploring how structures are linked to personal and relational racial dynamics.

- Cultivate curiosity about how organizations, policies, and practices might be creating or maintaining bias or inequality, even when that is not their explicit intention. Ask questions. Simply questioning disrupts business-as-usual and gives us the chance to learn more.
- If you feel powerless to make change in a situation, look at where you do have leverage in your life. Is there a small step you can take somewhere?
- Learn more about history. History provides perspective on how institutions have been shaped by the stratification of difference.

## Reflecting on Your Race-Related Learning

Learning about race and how to skillfully interact regarding racial matters is an ongoing journey. The following questions are for your reflection and for sharing in discussion with others committed to this learning journey. Start with a question that catches your attention or "speaks" to you. If a question doesn't make sense or resonate, allow yourself to move past it, but revisit it at another time to see if your relationship to the question has shifted. The questions are meant to be asked with kindness and curiosity, without judgment.

1. How open or resistant am I to new information?
2. What am I learning about how my identity has been shaped by race (along with gender, social class, and other social identities)?
3. How am I grappling with the structural disadvantage/advantage related to these social identities?
4. What am I beginning to see about how those who are racially different have been shaped by race?

5. What can I see about how interpersonal interactions are related to the larger social context?

6. How am I doing at holding awareness of multiple (sometimes contra-dictory) perspectives?

7. When I'm feeling defensive, am I able to look at what else is going on (that is, at related thoughts/beliefs)?

8. Am I able to compare and contrast different views about race?

9. How am I doing in handling uncertainty and not knowing?

10. What am I beginning to see about racial stereotypes and mistaken beliefs that I was previously unaware of?

11. Am I able to name ways in which race matters and ways in which it doesn't matter? Am I able to see both sameness and difference?

12. What sorts of things (such as ideas, comments from others, inter-actions, feelings) lead me to feel overwhelmed or discouraged?

13. Am I able to see how privilege shifts in different relationships and circumstances?

14. Can I be open to being curious, to living with questions about race? What does it mean to have a racial identity? How do we participate in creating race? What is an appropriate response in a race-related encounter? What is effective action to address racial disparities?

## Learning Activities for Exploring

### Interconnections Between Structural and Interpersonal Aspects of Race—Discrimination Relay

(With thanks to Erika Thorne of Training for Change, www.trainingforchange.org)

**Purpose:** To help increase understanding of the interconnections between individual and structural aspects of race; to see how lack of awareness of structures contributes to personal rather than situational attributions.

Supplies—A soup ladle, a soup spoon, peppercorns, twine or yarn, objects to create obstacles (trash can, stools or chairs, small tables, easel, whatever happens to be around)

Set Up—Create a course for the relay. Possibilities include creating long aisles on either side of a room, pushing desks or tables to the side to create a space in the center of a room, or using a hallway or the sidewalk outside a building. The relay area is marked off into two courses with the twine or yarn. Each course is the same length, but one will be very narrow and will have a number of obstacles in it.

*The teams.*

Depending on group size, randomly assign 6 to 15 people to each team, the A team and the Z team. Assign remaining people to be observers; they are specifically assigned to observe either the A team, the Z team, or the entire process. (Observers aren't absolutely necessary but are useful.)

*The activity.*

The A team is given the soup ladle with peppercorns in it; the Z team is given the soup spoon with peppercorns in it. In front of the entire group tell participants they will be taking part in the "Discrimination Relay," and give each team instructions that are named as "identical." The first team member from each team traverses the course as quickly as possible without spilling the peppercorns, then hands off to a member on the opposite end. That member runs back toward the start and hands off the spoon, and this is repeated until all members have traversed the length of the course. The A team is told to encourage and cheer for team members; the Z team is told they are not to talk or make eye contact. The Z team also needs to maneuver around and past obstacles, but the A team does not. The first team to finish wins the relay. As you might imagine, the A team always wins.

*Possible challenges.*

Sometimes team members will challenge the arrangements, saying that they do not appear fair or equal. Politely but firmly respond to these challenges. You will need to improvise! For example, you might deflect a critique by noting how important it is to think positively, to act with confidence and proceed to run the relay. Sometimes team members will break the rules during the relay. An A team member might, for example, remove an obstacle from the Z team's course. Allow the process to unfold, but make sure to discuss participants' interpretations. The A team member might have intended to be helpful, but a Z team member might not experience this behavior as helpful but as patronizing or arrogant instead.

*Debriefing.*

Start by asking the observers what they saw. (They usually describe the inequitable setup.) Ask team members what they experienced. A team members might have a range of responses, including that it was fun, that it felt good to win, and that it's nice to have it easy. They might also say that it wasn't fun because there was no genuine competition, and that it felt awkward to be so far ahead and to see how much harder the other team had to work. Sometimes A team members will take actions during the relay to intervene on behalf of the Z team. Z team members might also have a range of responses, including that it wasn't fun and felt unfair, that they gave up and didn't try hard because the outcome was obvious, that they redefined success as character building rather than winning, or that they started to feel bad about themselves because they were slow in navigating past obstacles. Sometimes a team will refuse to participate. Whether teams play by the rules or break them is not important to the success of the activity; either way, there will be plenty to discuss.

To explore attributions, ask observers how they interpreted what happened. For example, did they think that the A team members won because they were more athletic or smarter? Did the Z team lose because members were lazy or uncoordinated? It is possible to have a conversation about differences in interpretation and how, even under these contrived circumstances, participants can start to interpret their experience through the lens of personal identity characteristics.

This activity typically generates lots of different feelings. Make a space for participants to name their feelings and reflect on them. Here is a list of possible discussion questions:

1. Describe what you saw happen during the relay.
2. How do you understand what happened? How did you feel?
3. Is the set up of the discrimination relay similar to any situations in real life? If so, what are they?
4. If you challenged the rules, what was it like to do so? If no one challenged or broke the rules, how do you understand that?
5. When in your life have you overcome obstacles like those in the relay? What helped you do this?
6. If you are nice to the Z team, if you treat them respectfully, will it make a difference? How or in what ways does it make a difference? How or in what ways does it *not* make a difference?
7. What actions could be taken that would make a difference for the Z team?
8. Should you feel guilty for being on the A team? If you feel guilty about being on the A team, how or in what ways might this be helpful? How or in what ways might it be unhelpful?

## Community Mapping: Experience the Community

(With thanks to Kathleen Tindle, ktindle@gwu.edu)

**Purpose:** Community Mapping can be used to address gaps in teacher background knowledge and experience, or to freshly see taken-for-granted communities.

Community Mapping is a way to experience a community by walking through a defined "map" of the neighborhood and talking with people who live or work there. This can be especially important for teachers who teach in chronically high-poverty neighborhoods of the inner city but have never spent much time there. If you have no direct experience or knowledge of families with generational cycles of poverty or of communities with gang and drug violence and without access to books and grocery stores, you most likely will have unexplored implicit attitudes about students' potential and their families' lives.

By mindfully exploring a focused section of the community, the community reveals itself in multiple ways. Personally gathered information promotes awareness and appreciation of community issues, resources, businesses, services, and occupations. Talking with people on the street, on front porches or in businesses, promotes initial feelings of connection with community members. Physically walking the streets of a neighborhood helps teachers become physically comfortable with the neighborhood. If some feel afraid, it honors those feelings yet helps address fears in a positive, productive way.

*The activity.*

The Mapping process is structured for small interdependent working groups of up to five people, using input from all members as a means of developing a richer understanding that respects and values the community culture and that stays alert for potential personal bias.

*Before* the Community Mapping trip, your group will:

- Examine a map of a portion of the school community (preplanned by Mapping organizers already familiar with the community)
- Brainstorm places and people you might see

*During* the Community Mapping, you will *LEARN* more about:

- Organizations in the community
- Its geography and architecture

- Different kinds of businesses
- Issues or perceptions important to community members

*During* the Community Mapping, you will *DO* the following:

- Explore a special section of the community. Each group is assigned to a geographic area that highlights a particular aspect of the community. For example, one map area might be mostly housing and parks; another, businesses and boarded-up buildings; and another, churches and nonprofit organizations. As each group reports, the larger group learns about the community as a whole.
- Go on a scavenger hunt. This involves collecting "artifacts" representative of the area. Examples include flyers from churches and menus from restaurants. Conversations with business owners or people living in the area also count as "collectibles."
- Take photos and make observations.

*After* the Community Mapping, your group will:

- Return to the larger group and present initial impressions from the mapping (on Mapping day).
- Research the background of the community to round out your community knowledge (over the following month).
- Make a final (PowerPoint?) presentation to share with the larger group. Write a personal reflection about your preconceived ideas before Mapping and how Mapping validated and/or challenged those ideas.

## References

Bell, L. A. (2010). Learning through story types about race and racism: Preparing teachers for social justice. In K. Skubikowski, C. Wright, & R. Graf (Eds.), *Social justice education: Inviting faculty to transform their institutions.* Sterling, VA: Stylus.

Bonilla-Silva, E. (2003). *Racism without racists: Color-blind racism and the persistence of inequality in the United States.* Lanham, MD: Rowman & Littlefield.

Hartigan, J. Jr., (2010). *Race in the 21st century: Ethnographic approaches.* New York: Oxford University Press.

# CONTRIBUTORS

**Tara L. Affolter** is a visiting assistant professor of education studies at Middlebury College in Middlebury, Vermont. She has spent the bulk of her career in high school classrooms, teaching English and theater and working for social justice in public school systems. She is keenly interested in finding ways to build fully inclusive environments within schools, colleges, and universities.

**Sharon J. Barnett** is a licensed associate in marriage and family therapy (LAMFT) and currently provides mental health services to a culturally diverse population coping with the effects of serious and persistent mental illness. She earned her bachelor's degree in English from the University of Minnesota and her master's in marriage and family therapy from the University of Wisconsin at Stout. Sharon lives in Minneapolis with her female partner, two dogs, and their soon-to-be-born baby, who kicked and somersaulted with abandon the entire time she wrote her chapter.

**Bridget Christianson** grew up the third of four children in Livonia, Michigan, and graduated from Eastern Michigan University with a master's degree in education. She is a sports enthusiast and enjoys reading, teaching, and spending time with family and friends. Now in her 10th year of teaching elementary school in Romulus, Michigan, Bridget is living her dream of being a teacher—a dream she's had since she was a child.

**Tabitha Dell'Angelo**, PhD, is an assistant professor and coordinator of the urban education master's program at the College of New Jersey. Her research interests include cultural identity development, stress tolerance and coping strategies for teachers, and using improvisational acting in teacher preparation and teaching. She holds a doctorate in interdisciplinary studies in human development from the University of Pennsylvania and teaches courses in child and adolescent development, urban education, cultural foundations, and teacher research.

**Kat Griffith** has worked as an environmental educator in Costa Rica, an agricultural economist, a community organizer, a sustainable agriculture advocate, a writer, and for nine years, a home-schooling mom. She lives with her husband and children in east central Wisconsin, where she is currently a high school Spanish teacher.

**Judith M. James**, EdD, is a diversity consultant with her own company, Diversity Works. Her company facilitates the development of intercultural communications among different ethnic, racial, and cultural groups. Dr. James has worked in K–12 districts for more than 20 years as a teacher, staff development trainer, and administrator. She has also worked in higher education for the past seven years, teaching classes for educators and communication classes for students interested in becoming more interculturally competent. Besides her work in diversity, Judith is currently a test administrator for the University of Minnesota.

**Terri A. Karis**, PhD, is an associate professor in the marriage and family therapy program and department of human development and family studies at the University of Wisconsin at Stout. Licensed as a family therapist and a psychologist, she maintains a clinical practice in Minneapolis. Her scholarly interests include how students learn about race, how to have transformative conversations about race, and how interpersonal neurobiology applies to education and psychotherapy and education. She is a mother of two biracial young-adult sons.

**Julie Landsman** taught in the Minneapolis public schools for 25 years. She has taught at Carleton College and has been an adjunct professor at Hamline University in St. Paul as well as St. Thomas and Metro State. Her books *Basic Needs: A Year With Street Kids in a City School*; *A White Teacher Talks About Race*; and, most recently, *Growing Up White: A Veteran Teacher Reflects on Racism*, are memoirs about her days in Minneapolis Public Schools. She has coedited six books on race, culture, and education. Julie has been a featured speaker on White privilege in the United States and in other countries including Thailand, Sweden, and France. She is a firm believer in stories as the key to understanding.

**Nancy Peterson**, MEd, now retired, taught early childhood special education (ECSE) in Minneapolis Public Schools for 30 years. She writes poetry and memoir and has been part of an interracial family for 33 years. She is working on racial awareness and social justice in groups with the organization she cofounded, Winds of Change.

**Kat Richter**, an arts educator and freelance writer, divides her time between Philadelphia and London. Prior to completing her master's degree in dance anthropology, she performed as a principal dancer with the New Jersey Tap Ensemble and taught tap at Guilford Elementary School in Baltimore from 2006 through 2007. Richter teaches tap throughout the United States and the United Kingdom and regularly contributes to *Dance Teacher* magazine. She is working on her first book, and she blogs at www.katrichterwrites.wordpress.com.

**Peggy Semingson** is an assistant professor of curriculum and instruction at the University of Texas at Arlington in the College of Education and Health Professions, where she teaches graduate and undergraduate courses in literacy studies. Prior to this, she taught elementary school and was a bilingual reading specialist for a total of eight years in Southern California and Central Texas. She was recently awarded the Jeanne S. Chall Research Grant from Harvard University to pursue research on ways to assist upper-grade readers in reading instruction.

**Rachel Stephens** is a first-grade teacher in the Metro Detroit area. She has been teaching for the past eight years. Her greatest passion is working in low-income school districts. Rachel has earned both her bachelor's and master's degrees from Eastern Michigan University.

**Kathleen Tindle** is currently the program director for the Literacy Cooperative Program at the George Washington University (GWU) Graduate School of Education and Human Development. The Literacy Cooperative is an urban teacher preparation program that frames education as a social justice issue. Kathleen began her education career as a preschool special education assistant, became a 3rd- and 4th-grade elementary teacher, and then worked as a middle school science teacher for most of her 15 years of teaching. During her years teaching in middle schools Kathleen earned her master's degree from University of Maryland in curriculum and instruction, and she served as department chair, team leader, and informal mentor to novice teachers. She went on to formally study teacher support in GWU's curriculum and instruction doctoral program and was hired to lead the Urban Initiative program upon graduation. She has continued leading GWU's urban education initiatives since 2001.

discriminating tastes, 18–19
discrimination relay, 168–170
diversity
    first tastes of, 20–21
    inadequacy of curriculum, 3
    respect for, xi
    self in, 30–31
    training in, 84
dream job, pursuing, 6–7

education
    framing, as social justice, 41–43
    need for active involvement in, 95–98
    working with preservice teachers in
        framing as social justice, 41–43
egalitarianism, 19
elementary school, family stories and,
    133–134
emerging/transformative stories, use of, to
        challenge the security of silence by
        white women in schools, 1
emotional trauma, learning to handle, 36
empathy, innocent, 17, 19–20
English language learner (ELL) students
    academic level of, 50–51
    behavior of, 50–51
    crackdown with, 52–53
    creating opportunities for outside the
        classroom, 53–54
    discipline and, 51
    style of leadership with, 51–52
    teaching, 50
entitlement, 19
    race and, 46
excellent mistakes of teachers, 3
expectations, naïveté of my, 7–8, 9

failure, sidestepping, at Guilford Elementary
    School, 115–128
family
    changes in dynamic, 33–34
    giving love in, 17
*Family Matters* (television series), 5
family-of-origin dynamics, need for approval
    and, 47

*Family Pictures/Cuadros de Familia* (Garza),
    93
family stories
    culture and, 133
    elementary and middle school and,
        133–134
    high school and, 134–135
    toddlerhood and, 133
fears
    making mistakes out of, 81–84
    in talking about race, as White women,
        70–72
*The Federalist Papers,* 49
feelings, using, 156
feminist movement, convergence of, 21
flow writing, 3–4, 32, 98, 128, 139, 153
free writing. *See* flow writing
*Funds of Knowledge* (Moll and González), 91

Garza, Carmen Lomas, 93
generalizations, origin of, xi
Gleaners Food Bank, 58
González, N., 89, 91
Goudvis, A., 93
Grand Valley State University (GVSU),
        becoming aware of racial consciousness,
        58
Griffith, Kat, 45, 174
guests, students' treatment of, in schools,
        119–120
Guilford Elementary School, sidestepping
        failure at, 115–128

Harvey, S., 93
Head Start programs, 137–138
hero
    becoming a, 17
    myth of the lone, 141–153
high school
    clichés in, 19–20
    emulation of caste system in, 6
    family stories and, 134–135
Hmong people, characteristics of, 27
homeschooling, 47, 48
home visits, 95–98
Hope Network in Grand Rapids, 58

Thomas, Dylan, 110
Tindle, Kathleen, 33, 175
toddlerhood, family stories and, 133
*To Kill a Mockingbird* (Lee), 102, 103
tracking of students, 103
traditional gender roles, Alaska women's
    non-conformance to, 87–88
transformation, beginning of, 91–94

uncomfortable, becoming comfortable with
    being, 156
*Under Milk Wood* (Thomas), 110
urban area, teaching in, 57

velvet paintings, 18–32
    applying acrylic gouache, 24–26
    beginning to create, 20–21
    building up layers of color, 27–28
    cleaning surface with lint brush as I work,
        29–30
    finding opacity in colors, 26
    laying down base coat with airbrush,
        21–22
    laying out precut images, 23–24
    stretching velvet over 7 mm board, 21
    understanding acrylic velvet as forgiving
        and durable, 30–31
    using masks for creating picture basics,
        22–23
    visualizing the image to be put on, 19–20
    working from dark to light in, 28–29
victim, playing the, 15
Vietnamese people, characteristics of, 27
violence
    desegregation and, 34–35

as solution to anger, 35
voice in classroom, 87, 92–93
voluntary support groups, intent of, 2–3
vulnerable, defending the, 19–20

weak, compulsion to protect, 20
welcome, 37–38
white, middle class neighborhood, growing
    up in, 5–6
white bilingual educator, thoughts from,
    87–98
"The White Butterfly" (poem), 78–79
whiteness, efforts to de-center, 110
white students
    prestige and privilege for, in high school,
        6
    setting of rules and norms by, 6
white teachers
    lack of desire for, 60–62
    struggles of, in sharing spotlight, 101–114
white women
    fear of, in talking about race, 70–72
    use of emerging/transformative stories to
        challenge the security of silence by, in
        schools, 1
*"Why Are All the Black Kids Sitting Together
    in the Cafeteria?"* (Tatum), 13
Wilson, August, 104
*The Wiz*, 106–107
*The Wizard of Oz*, 106
writing
    flow, 3–4, 32, 98, 128, 139, 153

*Y no se lo trajo la tierral . . . And the Earth
    Did Not Devour Him* (Rivera), 92